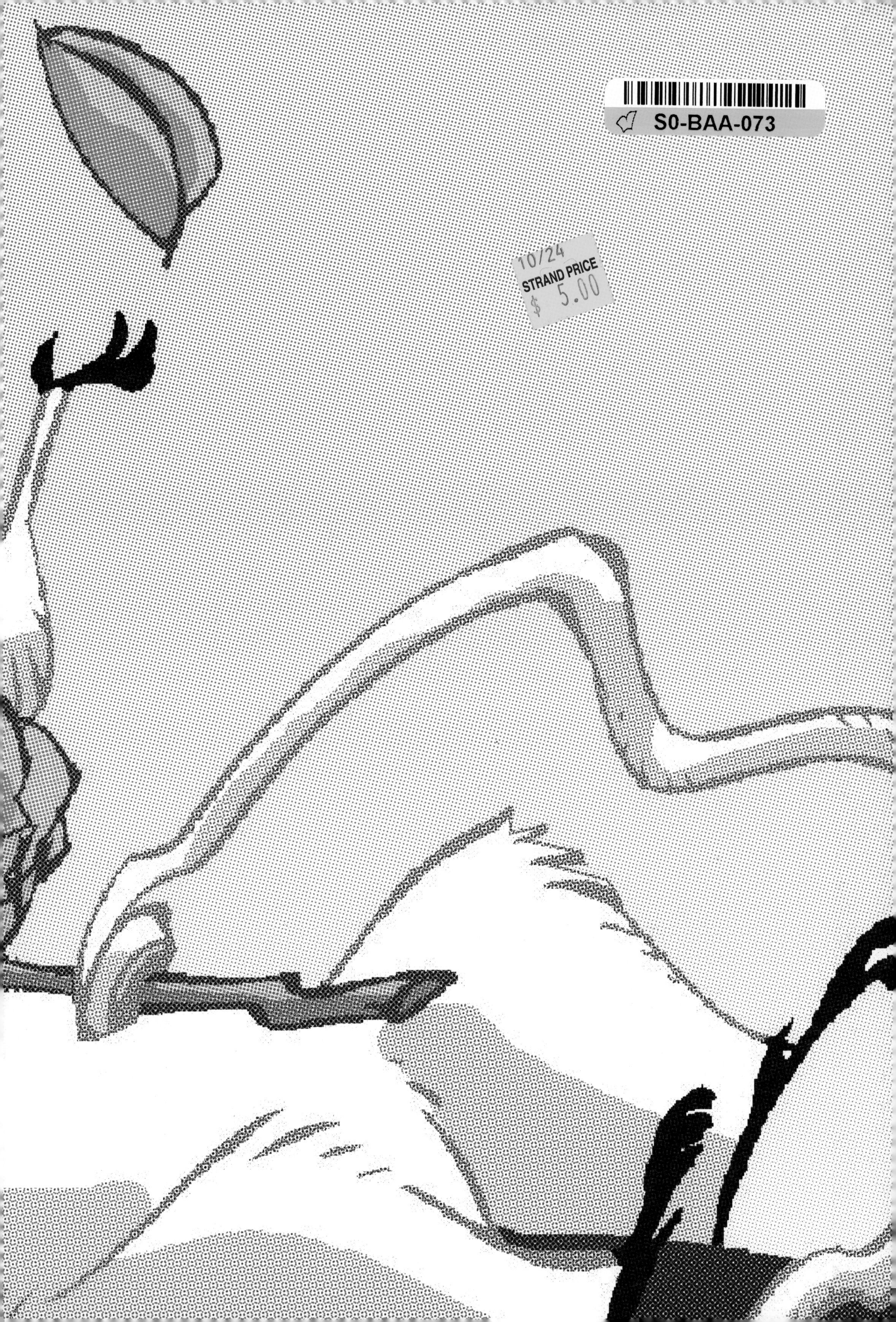

CARLOS TRILLO   JUAN BOBILLO

Case Two: The Sorcerer

Venture

DARK HORSE COMICS · STRIP ART FEATURES

Carlos Trillo • Juan Bobillo
ZACHARY HOLMES
Case Two - The Sorcerer

© Strip Art Features, 2002, www.safcomics.com

Published by
DARK HORSE COMICS, Inc.
10956 SE Main Street
Milwaukie, Oregon 97222, USA
www.darkhorse.com

First edition: April 2002
ISBN: 1-56971-703-6

Printed in Slovenia by SAF - Tiskarna Koper

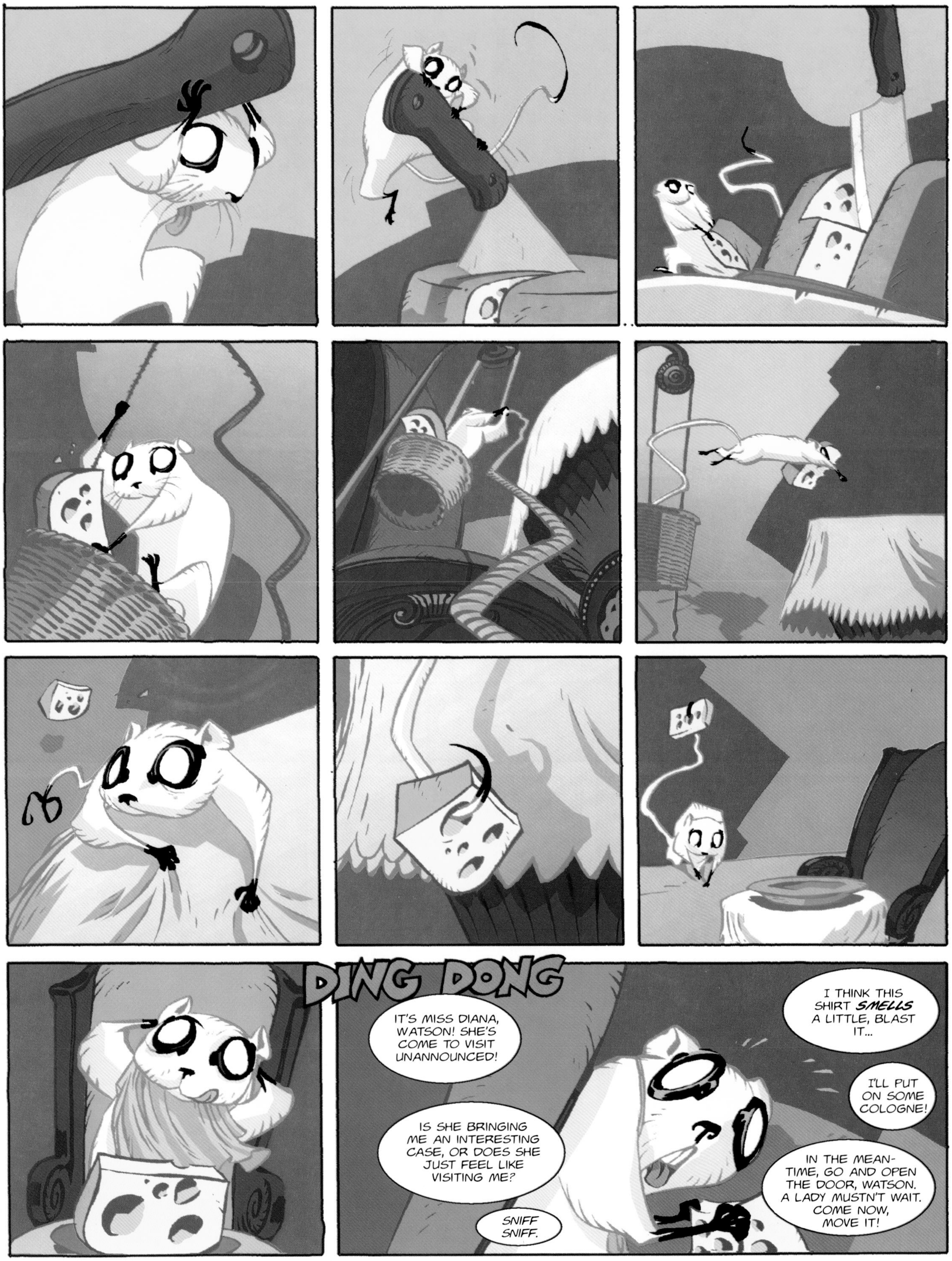
DING DONG
IT'S MISS DIANA, WATSON! SHE'S COME TO VISIT UNANNOUNCED!
IS SHE BRINGING ME AN INTERESTING CASE, OR DOES SHE JUST FEEL LIKE VISITING ME?
SNIFF SNIFF.
I THINK THIS SHIRT SMELLS A LITTLE, BLAST IT...
I'LL PUT ON SOME COLOGNE!
IN THE MEAN-TIME, GO AND OPEN THE DOOR, WATSON. A LADY MUSTN'T WAIT. COME NOW, MOVE IT!

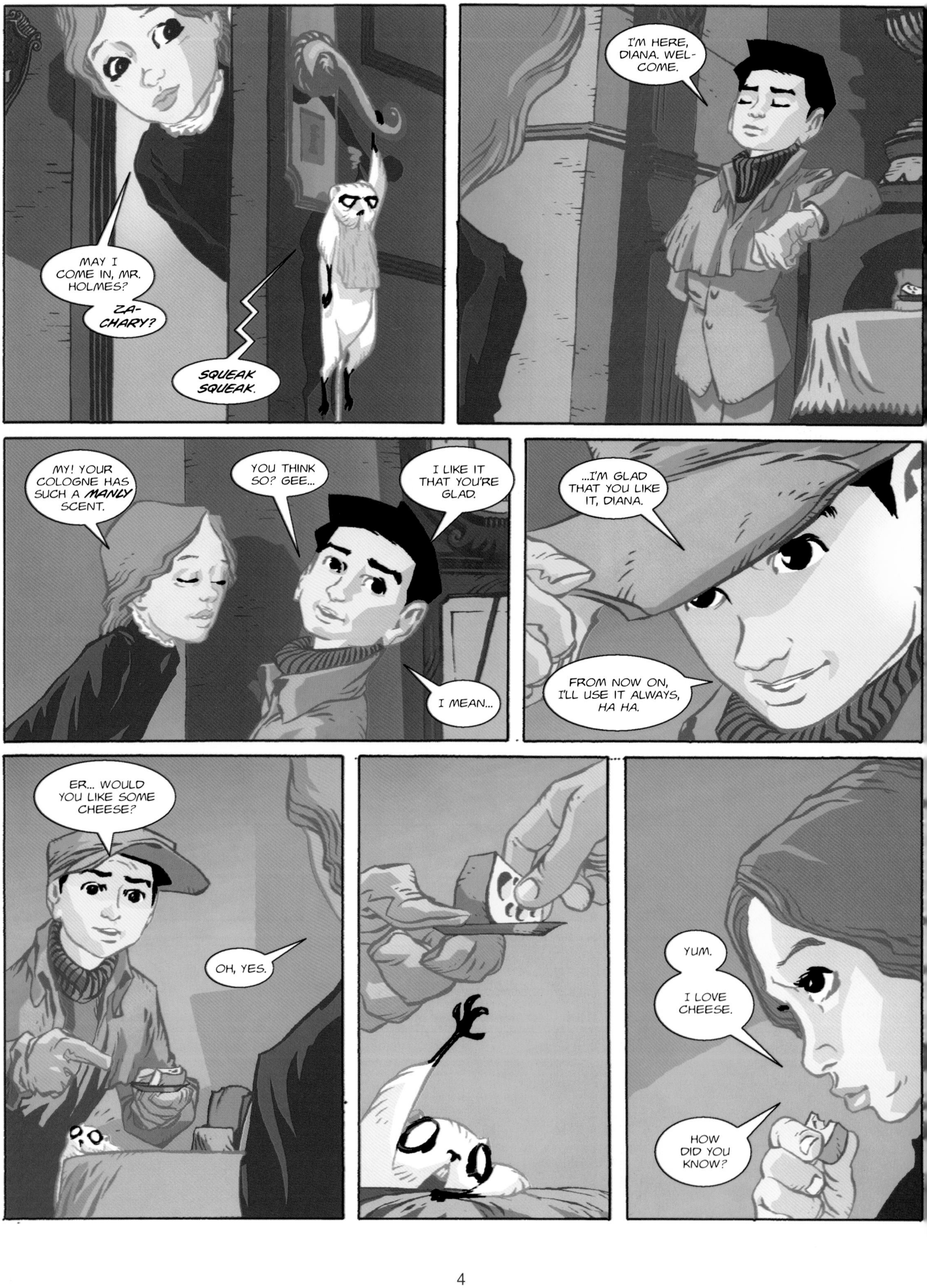
MAY I COME IN, MR. HOLMES?
ZA-CHARY?
SQUEAK SQUEAK.
I'M HERE, DIANA. WEL-COME.
MY! YOUR COLOGNE HAS SUCH A *MANLY* SCENT.
YOU THINK SO? GEE...
I LIKE IT THAT YOU'RE GLAD.
I MEAN...
...I'M GLAD THAT YOU LIKE IT, DIANA.
FROM NOW ON, I'LL USE IT ALWAYS, *HA HA.*
ER... WOULD YOU LIKE SOME CHEESE?
OH, YES.
YUM.
I LOVE CHEESE.
HOW DID YOU KNOW?

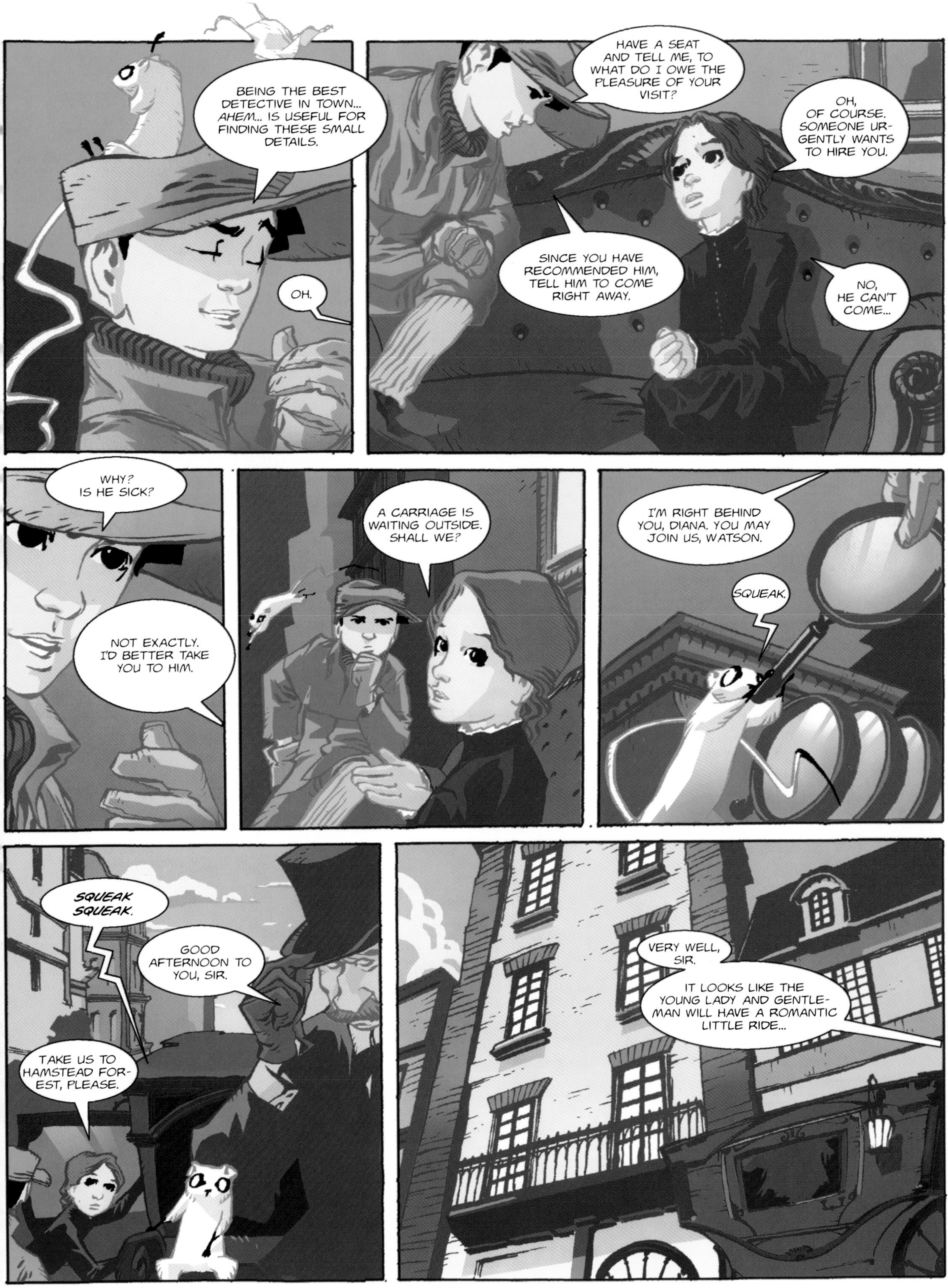
BEING THE BEST DETECTIVE IN TOWN... AHEM... IS USEFUL FOR FINDING THESE SMALL DETAILS.
OH.
HAVE A SEAT AND TELL ME, TO WHAT DO I OWE THE PLEASURE OF YOUR VISIT?
OH, OF COURSE. SOMEONE URGENTLY WANTS TO HIRE YOU.
SINCE YOU HAVE RECOMMENDED HIM, TELL HIM TO COME RIGHT AWAY.
NO, HE CAN'T COME...
WHY? IS HE SICK?
NOT EXACTLY. I'D BETTER TAKE YOU TO HIM.
A CARRIAGE IS WAITING OUTSIDE. SHALL WE?
I'M RIGHT BEHIND YOU, DIANA. YOU MAY JOIN US, WATSON.
SQUEAK.
SQUEAK SQUEAK.
GOOD AFTERNOON TO YOU, SIR.
TAKE US TO HAMSTEAD FOREST, PLEASE.
VERY WELL, SIR.
IT LOOKS LIKE THE YOUNG LADY AND GENTLEMAN WILL HAVE A ROMANTIC LITTLE RIDE...

STOP THE CARRIAGE!
WAIT HERE FOR US.
VERY WELL, MISS.
ARE YOU GOING WITH THEM, SIR?
SQUEAK. SQUEAK?
LOVERS' WALKS ARE USUALLY TAKEN IN TWOS, NOT THREES, SIR.
WATSON! COME ALONG! WHAT'S WRONG WITH YOU? DID YOU FALL ASLEEP?
DOES THE PERSON WHO NEEDS MY SERVICES LIVE NEARBY?
YES, HE DOES.
EXCUSE MY SUDDEN SHORT-SIGHTEDNESS, DIANA, BUT I SEE ONLY A TREE THERE.
THAT'S RIGHT, BOY! IT IS I WHO NEEDS YOUR HELP!
GULP.
SQUEAK.

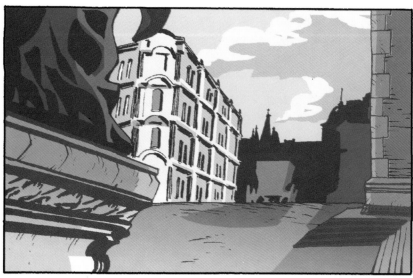

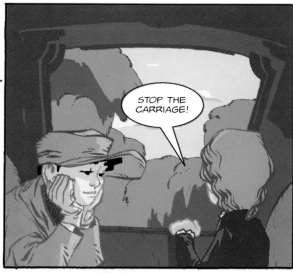

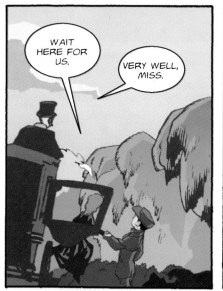

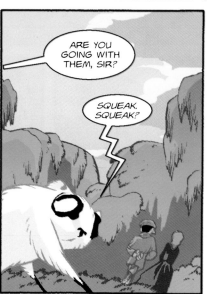

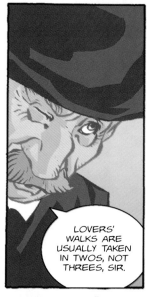

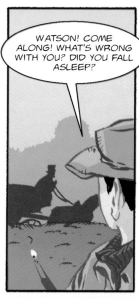

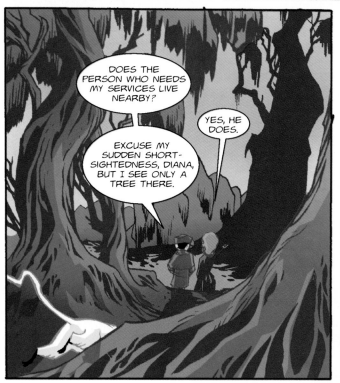

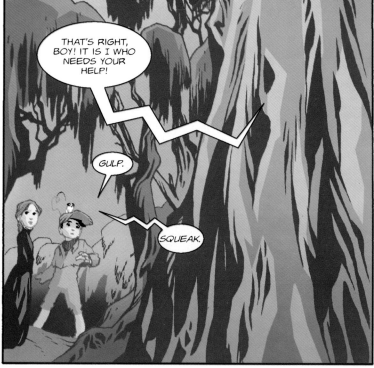

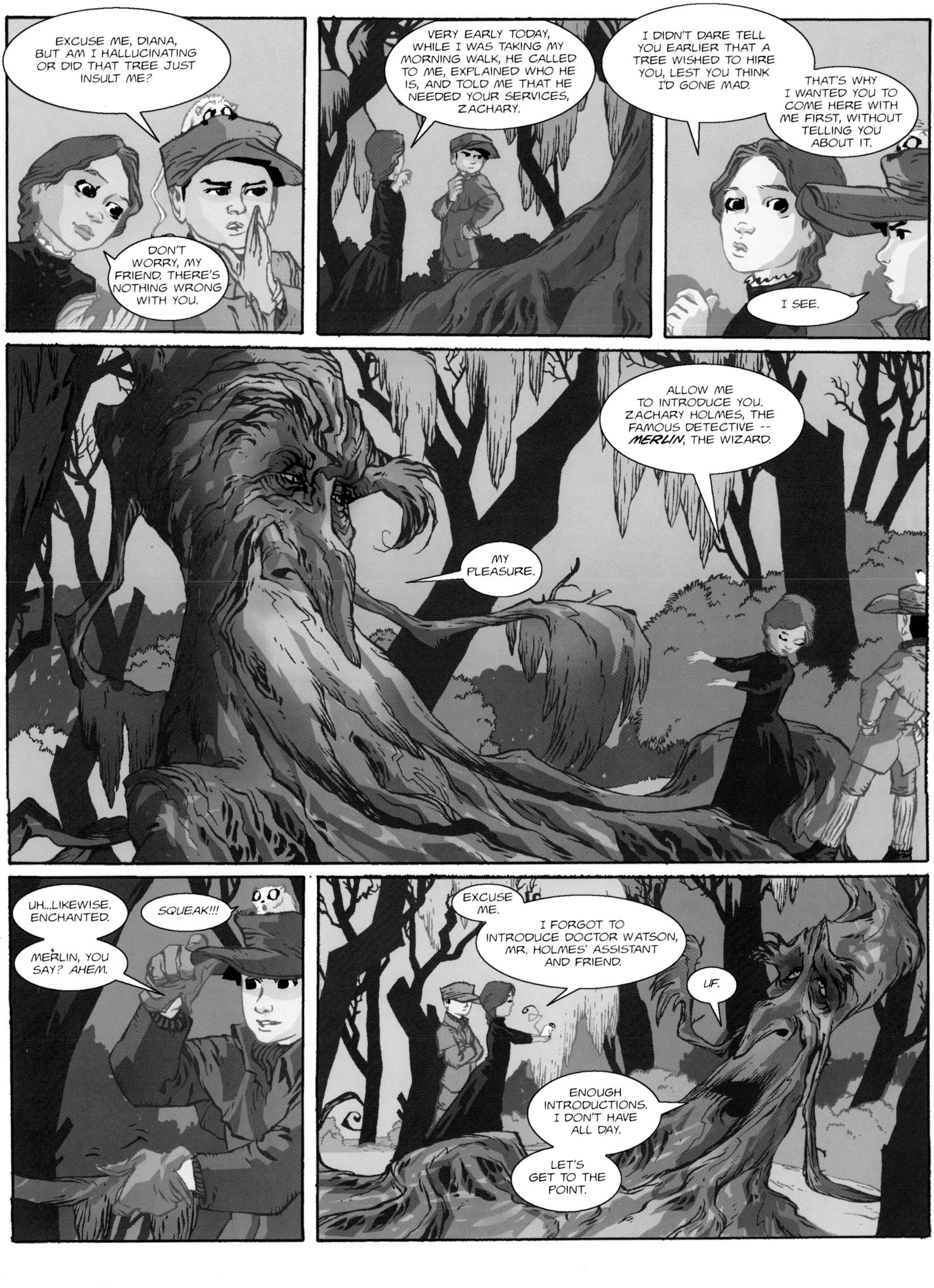
EXCUSE ME, DIANA, BUT AM I HALLUCINATING OR DID THAT TREE JUST INSULT ME?
DON'T WORRY, MY FRIEND. THERE'S NOTHING WRONG WITH YOU.
VERY EARLY TODAY, WHILE I WAS TAKING MY MORNING WALK, HE CALLED TO ME, EXPLAINED WHO HE IS, AND TOLD ME THAT HE NEEDED YOUR SERVICES, ZACHARY.
I DIDN'T DARE TELL YOU EARLIER THAT A TREE WISHED TO HIRE YOU, LEST YOU THINK I'D GONE MAD.
THAT'S WHY I WANTED YOU TO COME HERE WITH ME FIRST, WITHOUT TELLING YOU ABOUT IT.
I SEE.
ALLOW ME TO INTRODUCE YOU. ZACHARY HOLMES, THE FAMOUS DETECTIVE -- MERLIN, THE WIZARD.
MY PLEASURE.
UH...LIKEWISE. ENCHANTED.
SQUEAK!!!
MERLIN, YOU SAY? AHEM.
EXCUSE ME.
I FORGOT TO INTRODUCE DOCTOR WATSON, MR. HOLMES' ASSISTANT AND FRIEND.
UF.
ENOUGH INTRODUCTIONS. I DON'T HAVE ALL DAY.
LET'S GET TO THE POINT.

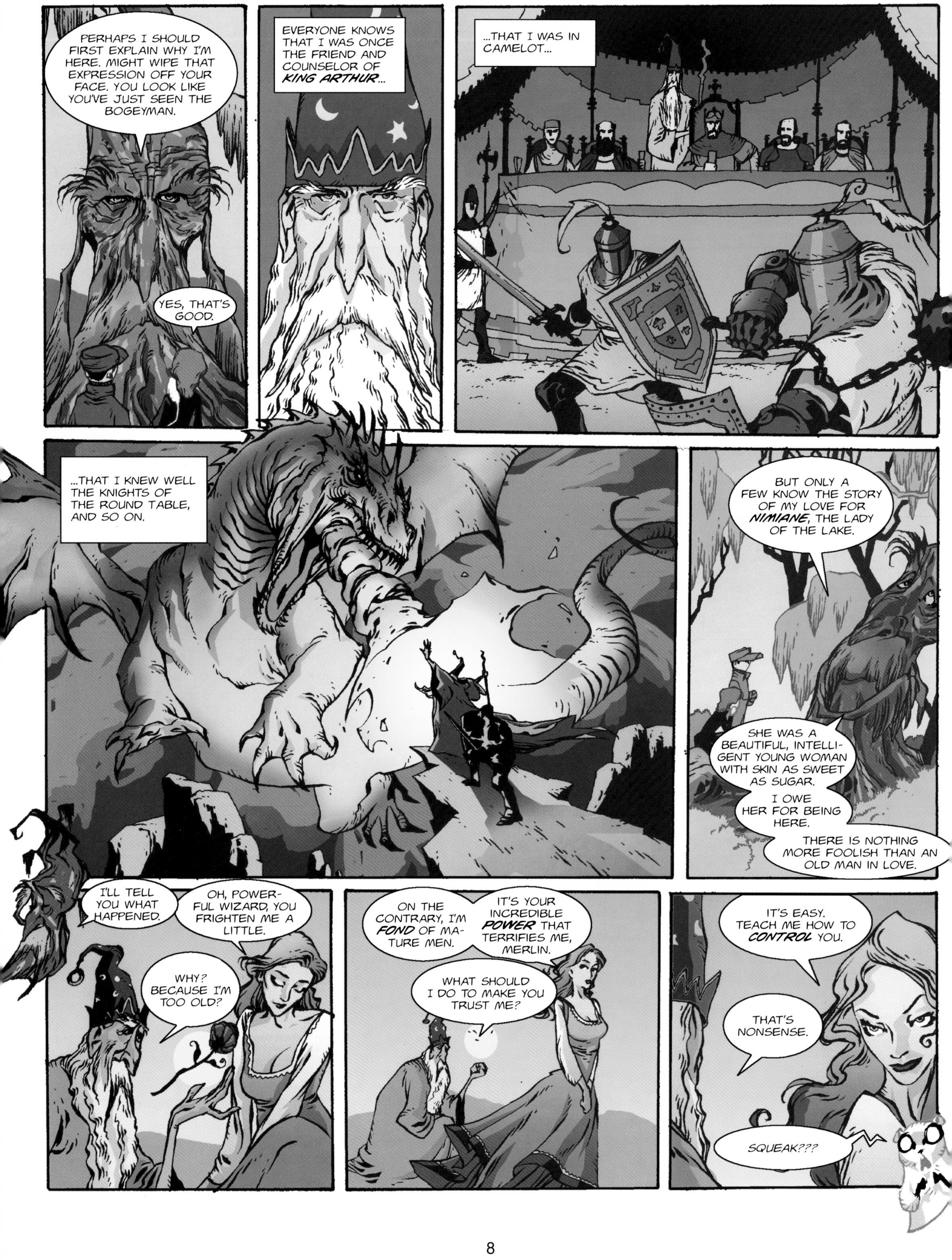
PERHAPS I SHOULD FIRST EXPLAIN WHY I'M HERE. MIGHT WIPE THAT EXPRESSION OFF YOUR FACE. YOU LOOK LIKE YOU'VE JUST SEEN THE BOGEYMAN.
YES, THAT'S GOOD.
EVERYONE KNOWS THAT I WAS ONCE THE FRIEND AND COUNSELOR OF KING ARTHUR...
...THAT I WAS IN CAMELOT...
...THAT I KNEW WELL THE KNIGHTS OF THE ROUND TABLE, AND SO ON.
BUT ONLY A FEW KNOW THE STORY OF MY LOVE FOR NIMIANE, THE LADY OF THE LAKE.
SHE WAS A BEAUTIFUL, INTELLIGENT YOUNG WOMAN WITH SKIN AS SWEET AS SUGAR.
I OWE HER FOR BEING HERE.
THERE IS NOTHING MORE FOOLISH THAN AN OLD MAN IN LOVE.
I'LL TELL YOU WHAT HAPPENED.
OH, POWERFUL WIZARD, YOU FRIGHTEN ME A LITTLE.
WHY? BECAUSE I'M TOO OLD?
ON THE CONTRARY, I'M FOND OF MATURE MEN.
IT'S YOUR INCREDIBLE POWER THAT TERRIFIES ME, MERLIN.
WHAT SHOULD I DO TO MAKE YOU TRUST ME?
IT'S EASY. TEACH ME HOW TO CONTROL YOU.
THAT'S NONSENSE.
SQUEAK???

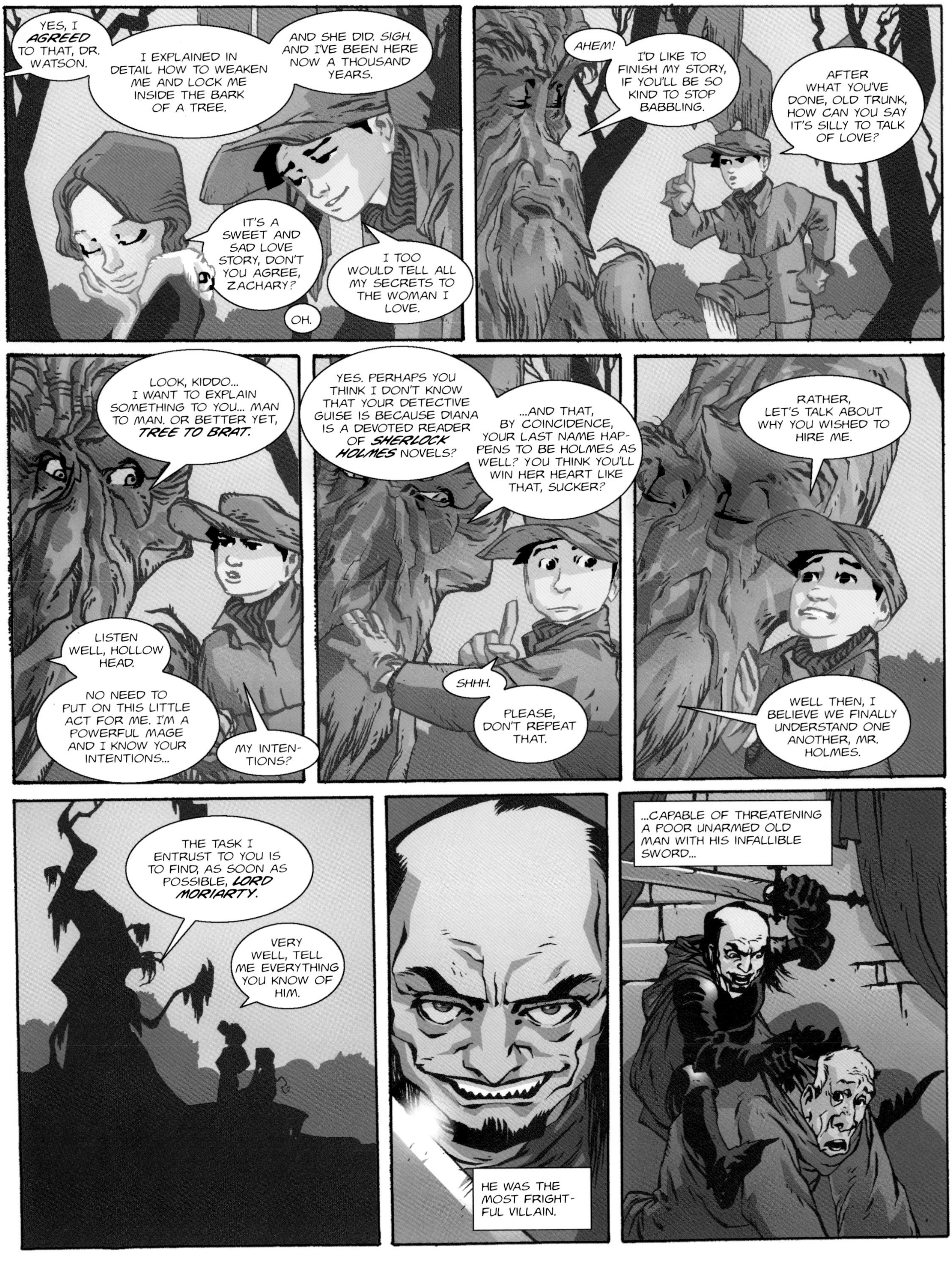
YES, I AGREED TO THAT, DR. WATSON.
I EXPLAINED IN DETAIL HOW TO WEAKEN ME AND LOCK ME INSIDE THE BARK OF A TREE.
AND SHE DID. SIGH. AND I'VE BEEN HERE NOW A THOUSAND YEARS.
IT'S A SWEET AND SAD LOVE STORY, DON'T YOU AGREE, ZACHARY?
I TOO WOULD TELL ALL MY SECRETS TO THE WOMAN I LOVE.
OH.
AHEM!
I'D LIKE TO FINISH MY STORY, IF YOU'LL BE SO KIND TO STOP BABBLING.
AFTER WHAT YOU'VE DONE, OLD TRUNK, HOW CAN YOU SAY IT'S SILLY TO TALK OF LOVE?
LOOK, KIDDO... I WANT TO EXPLAIN SOMETHING TO YOU... MAN TO MAN. OR BETTER YET, TREE TO BRAT.
LISTEN WELL, HOLLOW HEAD.
NO NEED TO PUT ON THIS LITTLE ACT FOR ME. I'M A POWERFUL MAGE AND I KNOW YOUR INTENTIONS...
MY INTENTIONS?
YES. PERHAPS YOU THINK I DON'T KNOW THAT YOUR DETECTIVE GUISE IS BECAUSE DIANA IS A DEVOTED READER OF SHERLOCK HOLMES NOVELS?
...AND THAT, BY COINCIDENCE, YOUR LAST NAME HAPPENS TO BE HOLMES AS WELL? YOU THINK YOU'LL WIN HER HEART LIKE THAT, SUCKER?
SHHH.
PLEASE, DON'T REPEAT THAT.
RATHER, LET'S TALK ABOUT WHY YOU WISHED TO HIRE ME.
WELL THEN, I BELIEVE WE FINALLY UNDERSTAND ONE ANOTHER, MR. HOLMES.
THE TASK I ENTRUST TO YOU IS TO FIND, AS SOON AS POSSIBLE, LORD MORIARTY.
VERY WELL, TELL ME EVERYTHING YOU KNOW OF HIM.
HE WAS THE MOST FRIGHTFUL VILLAIN.
...CAPABLE OF THREATENING A POOR UNARMED OLD MAN WITH HIS INFALLIBLE SWORD...

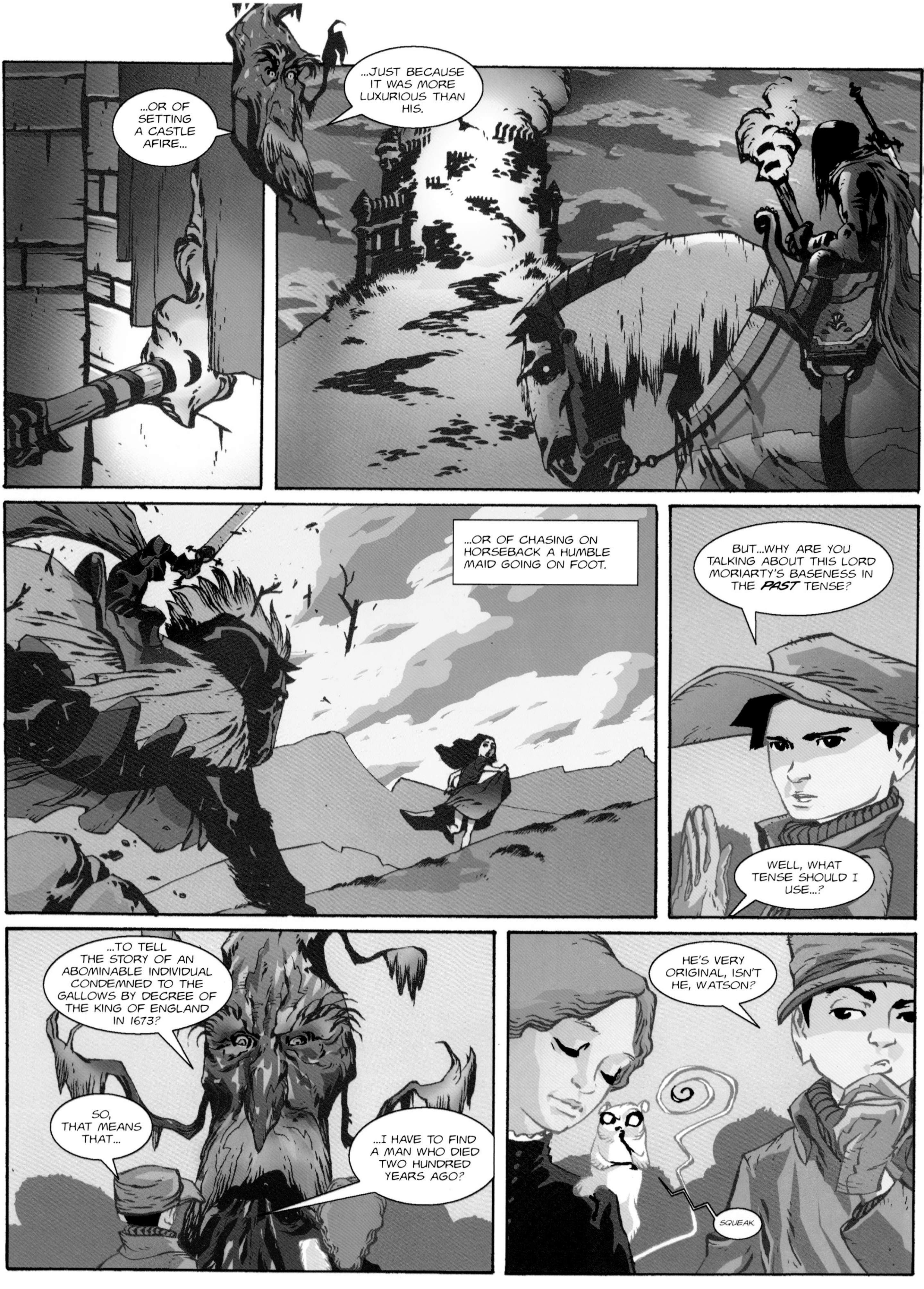
...OR OF SETTING A CASTLE AFIRE...
...JUST BECAUSE IT WAS MORE LUXURIOUS THAN HIS.
...OR OF CHASING ON HORSEBACK A HUMBLE MAID GOING ON FOOT.
BUT...WHY ARE YOU TALKING ABOUT THIS LORD MORIARTY'S BASENESS IN THE PAST TENSE?
WELL, WHAT TENSE SHOULD I USE...?
...TO TELL THE STORY OF AN ABOMINABLE INDIVIDUAL CONDEMNED TO THE GALLOWS BY DECREE OF THE KING OF ENGLAND IN 1673?
SO, THAT MEANS THAT...
...I HAVE TO FIND A MAN WHO DIED TWO HUNDRED YEARS AGO?
HE'S VERY ORIGINAL, ISN'T HE, WATSON?
SQUEAK.

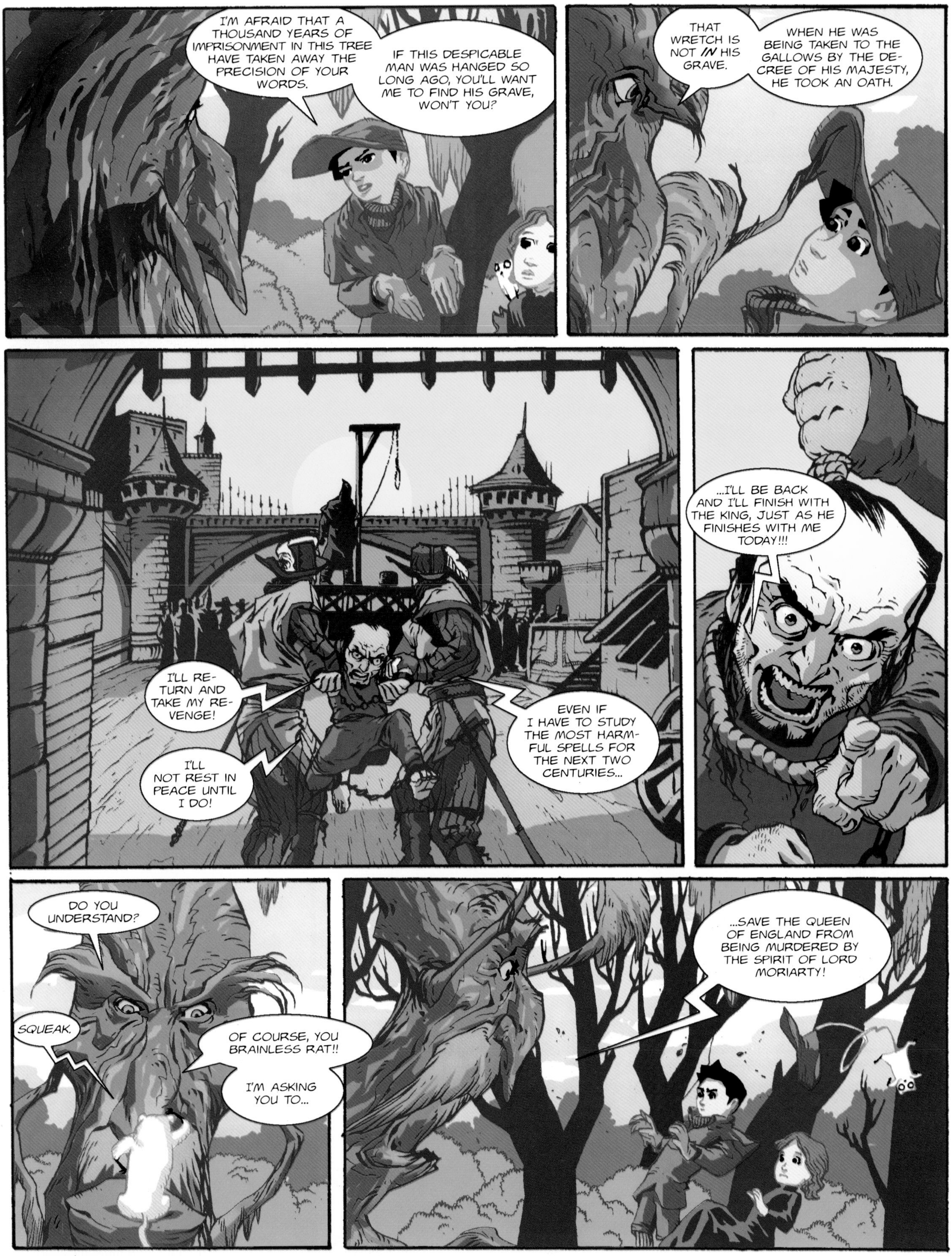

I'M AFRAID THAT A THOUSAND YEARS OF IMPRISONMENT IN THIS TREE HAVE TAKEN AWAY THE PRECISION OF YOUR WORDS.
IF THIS DESPICABLE MAN WAS HANGED SO LONG AGO, YOU'LL WANT ME TO FIND HIS GRAVE, WON'T YOU?
THAT WRETCH IS NOT *IN* HIS GRAVE.
WHEN HE WAS BEING TAKEN TO THE GALLOWS BY THE DECREE OF HIS MAJESTY, HE TOOK AN OATH.
I'LL RETURN AND TAKE MY REVENGE!
I'LL NOT REST IN PEACE UNTIL I DO!
EVEN IF I HAVE TO STUDY THE MOST HARMFUL SPELLS FOR THE NEXT TWO CENTURIES...
...I'LL BE BACK AND I'LL FINISH WITH THE KING, JUST AS HE FINISHES WITH ME TODAY!!!
DO YOU UNDERSTAND?
SQUEAK.
OF COURSE, YOU BRAINLESS RAT!!
I'M ASKING YOU TO...
...SAVE THE QUEEN OF ENGLAND FROM BEING MURDERED BY THE SPIRIT OF LORD MORIARTY!

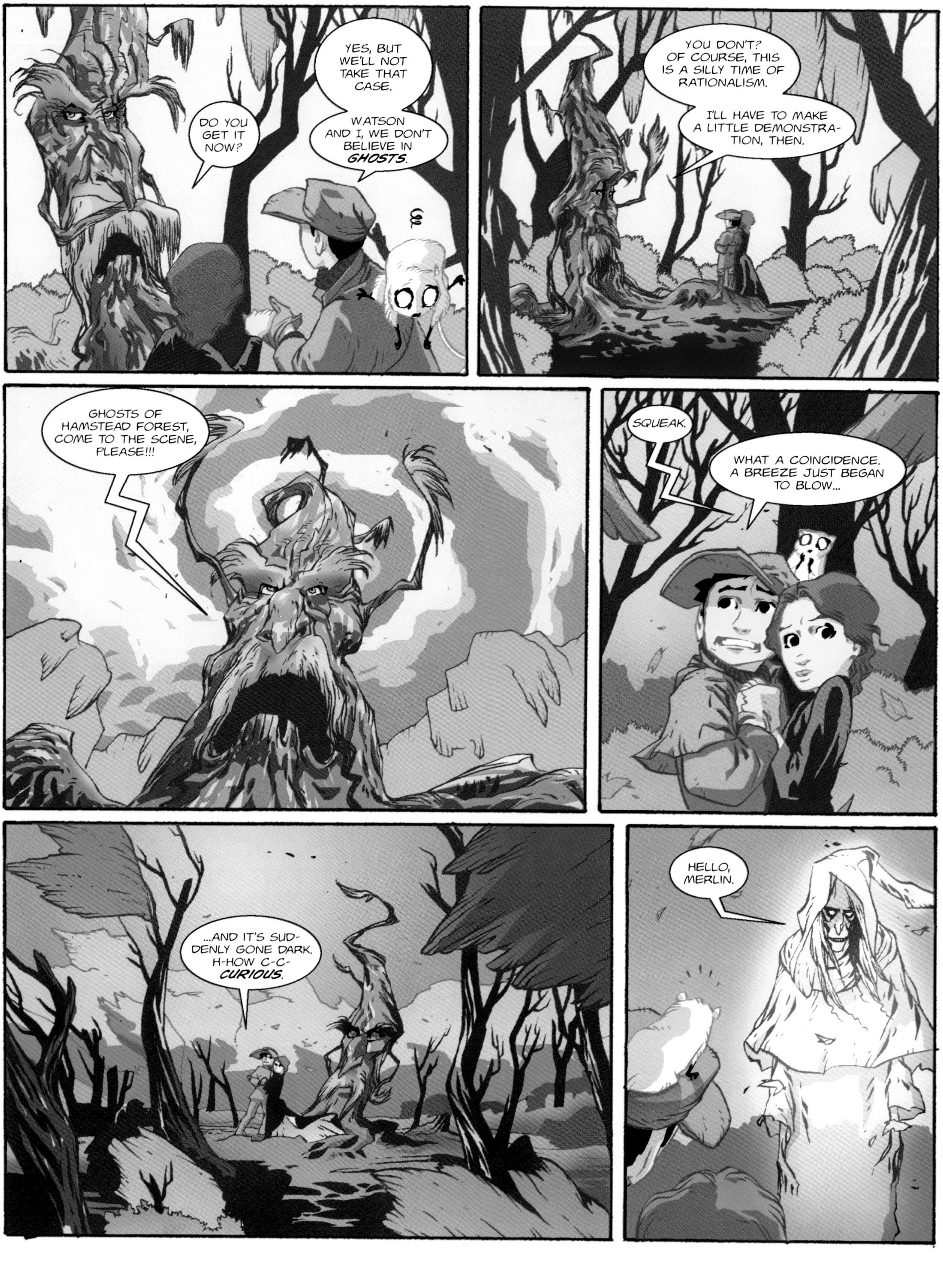

DO YOU GET IT NOW?
YES, BUT WE'LL NOT TAKE THAT CASE.
WATSON AND I, WE DON'T BELIEVE IN GHOSTS.
YOU DON'T? OF COURSE, THIS IS A SILLY TIME OF RATIONALISM.
I'LL HAVE TO MAKE A LITTLE DEMONSTRATION, THEN.
GHOSTS OF HAMSTEAD FOREST, COME TO THE SCENE, PLEASE!!!
SQUEAK.
WHAT A COINCIDENCE. A BREEZE JUST BEGAN TO BLOW...
...AND IT'S SUDDENLY GONE DARK. H-HOW C-C-CURIOUS.
HELLO, MERLIN.

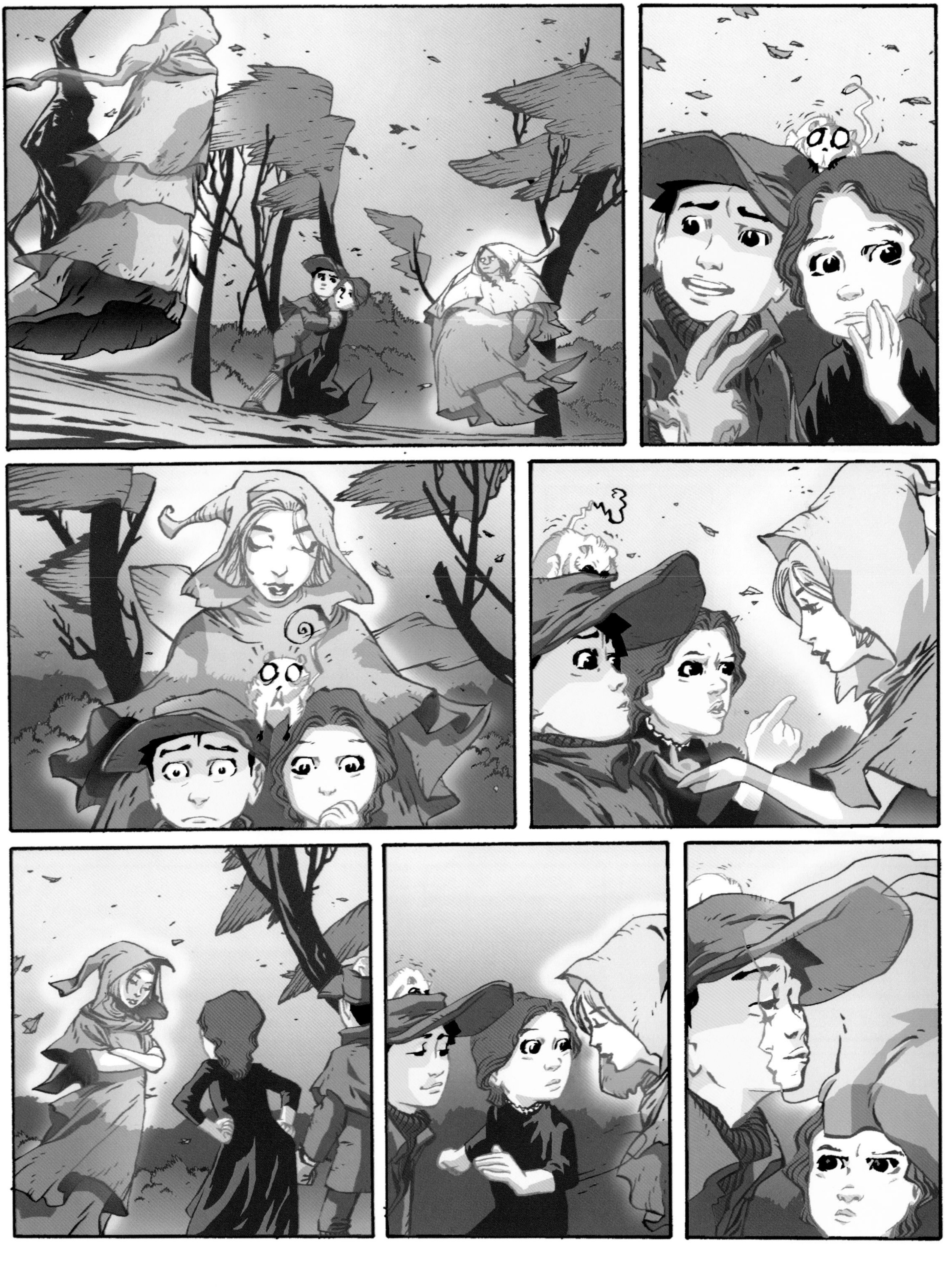

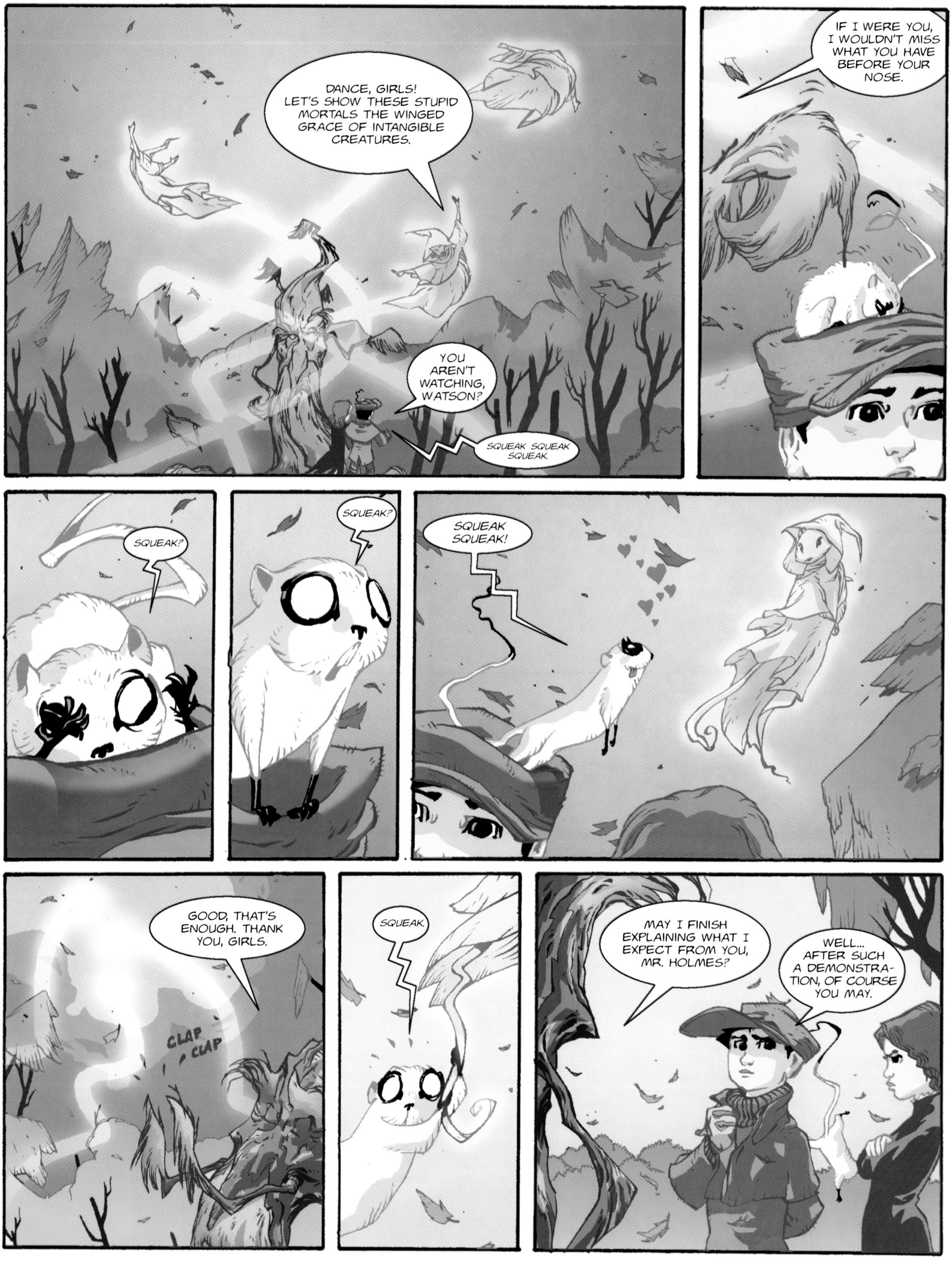

DANCE, GIRLS! LET'S SHOW THESE STUPID MORTALS THE WINGED GRACE OF INTANGIBLE CREATURES.
YOU AREN'T WATCHING, WATSON?
SQUEAK SQUEAK SQUEAK.
IF I WERE YOU, I WOULDN'T MISS WHAT YOU HAVE BEFORE YOUR NOSE.
SQUEAK?
SQUEAK?
SQUEAK SQUEAK!
GOOD, THAT'S ENOUGH. THANK YOU, GIRLS.
CLAP CLAP
SQUEAK.
MAY I FINISH EXPLAINING WHAT I EXPECT FROM YOU, MR. HOLMES?
WELL... AFTER SUCH A DEMONSTRA-TION, OF COURSE YOU MAY.

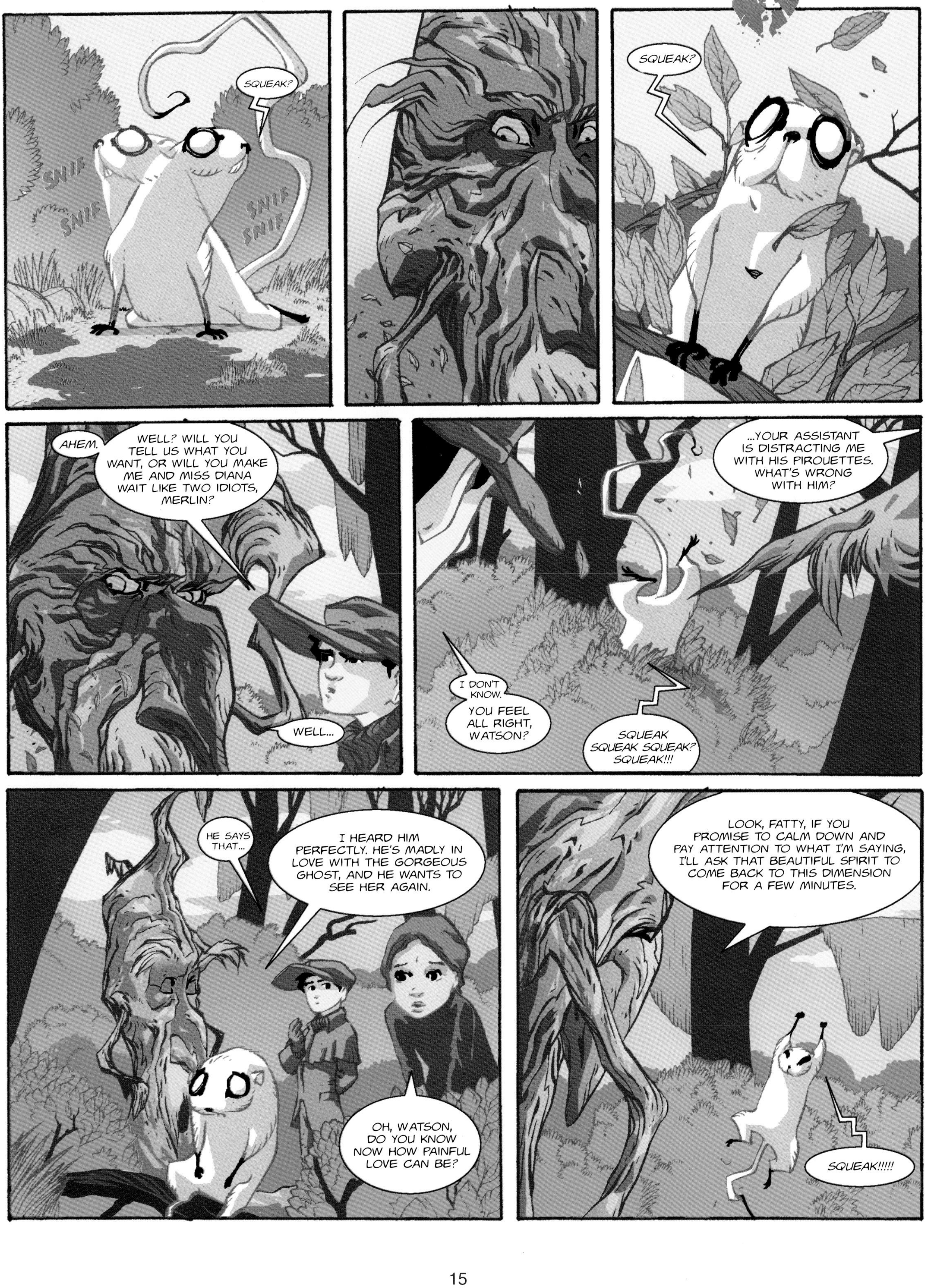

SQUEAK?
SNIF SNIF
SNIF SNIF
SQUEAK?
AHEM.
WELL? WILL YOU TELL US WHAT YOU WANT, OR WILL YOU MAKE ME AND MISS DIANA WAIT LIKE TWO IDIOTS, MERLIN?
WELL...
...YOUR ASSISTANT IS DISTRACTING ME WITH HIS PIROUETTES. WHAT'S WRONG WITH HIM?
I DON'T KNOW.
YOU FEEL ALL RIGHT, WATSON?
SQUEAK SQUEAK SQUEAK? SQUEAK!!!
HE SAYS THAT...
I HEARD HIM PERFECTLY. HE'S MADLY IN LOVE WITH THE GORGEOUS GHOST, AND HE WANTS TO SEE HER AGAIN.
OH, WATSON, DO YOU KNOW NOW HOW PAINFUL LOVE CAN BE?
LOOK, FATTY, IF YOU PROMISE TO CALM DOWN AND PAY ATTENTION TO WHAT I'M SAYING, I'LL ASK THAT BEAUTIFUL SPIRIT TO COME BACK TO THIS DIMENSION FOR A FEW MINUTES.
SQUEAK!!!!!

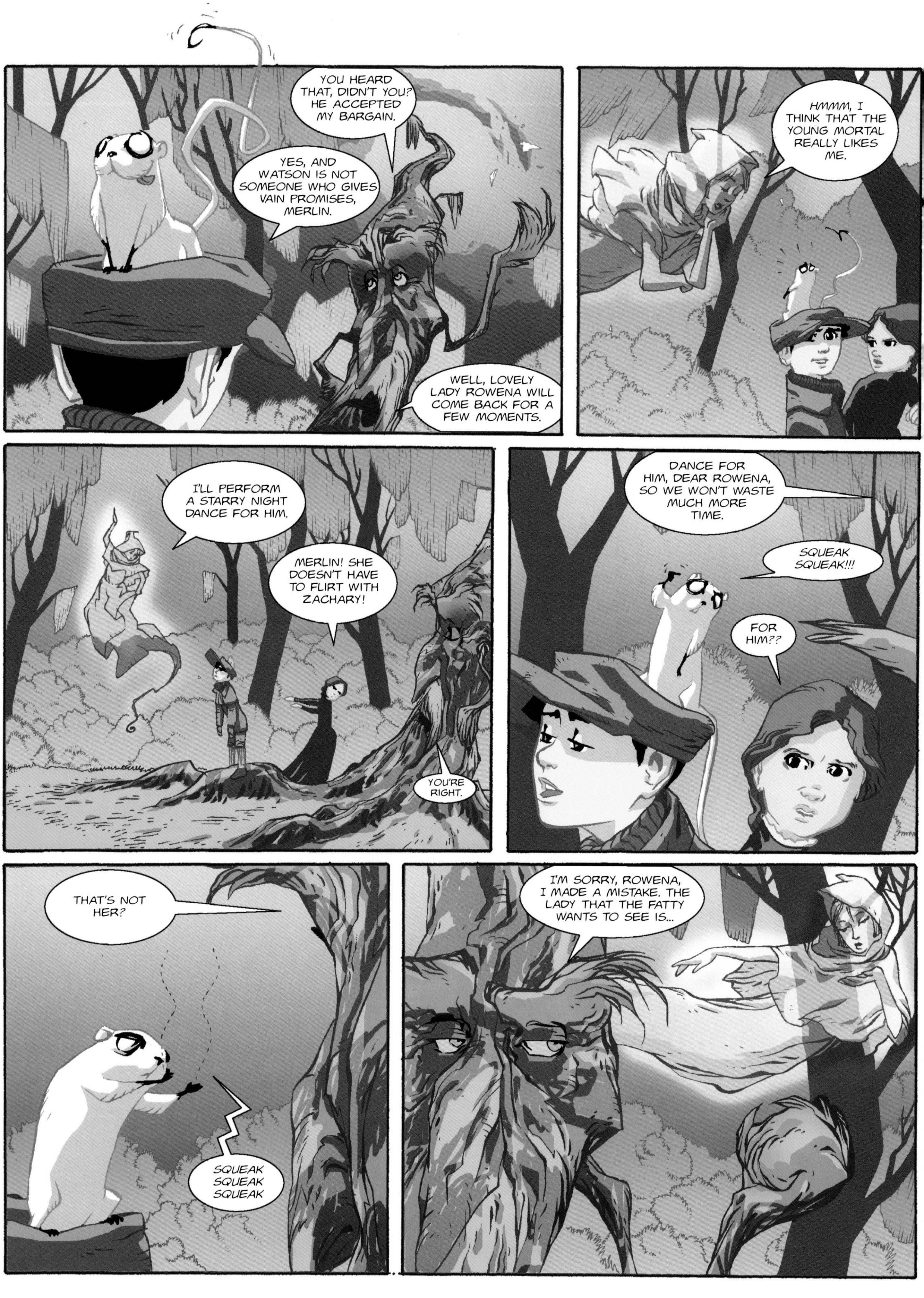
YOU HEARD THAT, DIDN'T YOU? HE ACCEPTED MY BARGAIN.
YES, AND WATSON IS NOT SOMEONE WHO GIVES VAIN PROMISES, MERLIN.
WELL, LOVELY LADY ROWENA WILL COME BACK FOR A FEW MOMENTS.
HMMM, I THINK THAT THE YOUNG MORTAL REALLY LIKES ME.
I'LL PERFORM A STARRY NIGHT DANCE FOR HIM.
MERLIN! SHE DOESN'T HAVE TO FLIRT WITH ZACHARY!
YOU'RE RIGHT.
DANCE FOR HIM, DEAR ROWENA, SO WE WON'T WASTE MUCH MORE TIME.
SQUEAK SQUEAK!!!
FOR HIM??
THAT'S NOT HER?
SQUEAK SQUEAK SQUEAK
I'M SORRY, ROWENA, I MADE A MISTAKE. THE LADY THAT THE FATTY WANTS TO SEE IS...

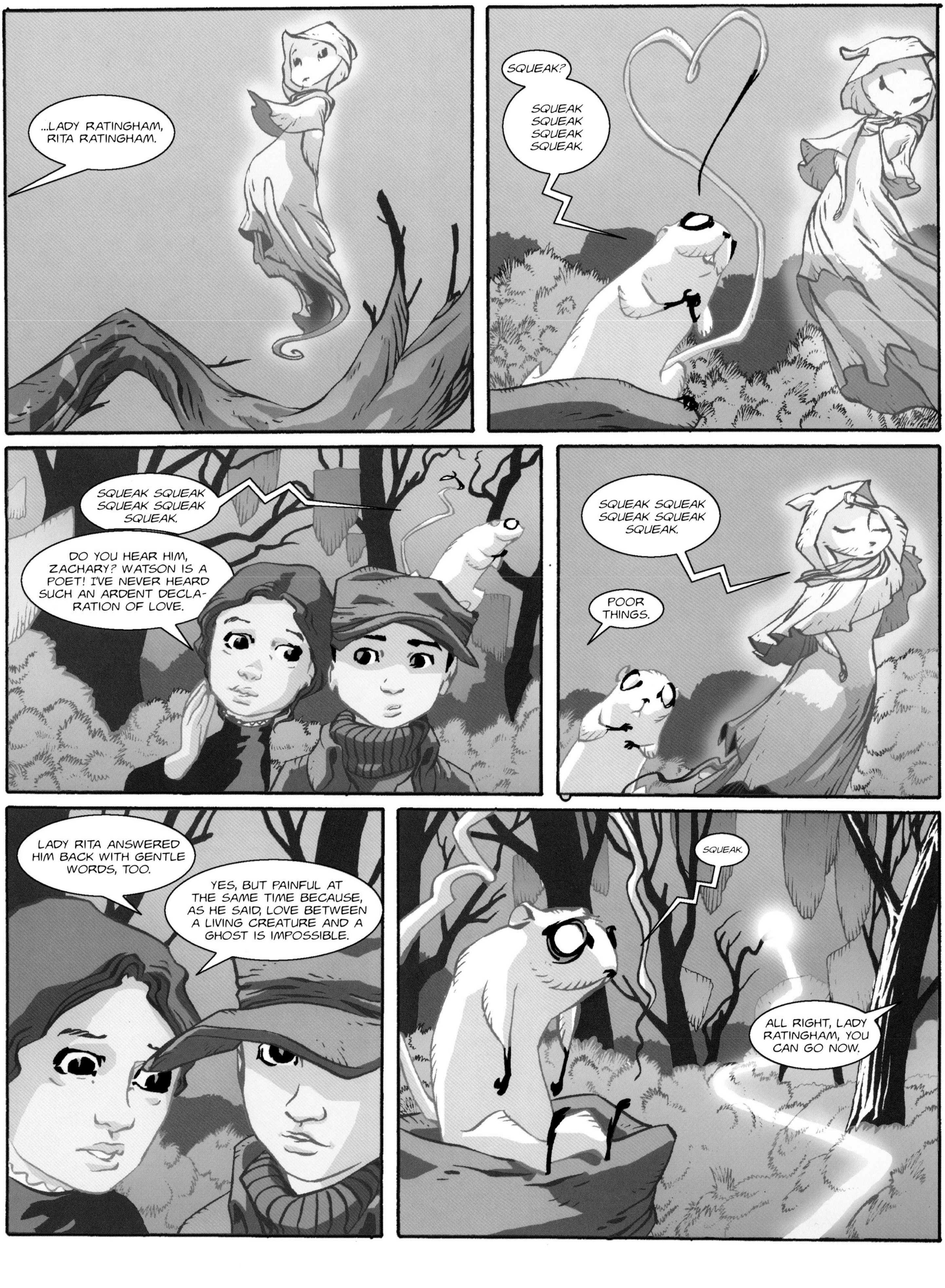
...LADY RATINGHAM, RITA RATINGHAM.
SQUEAK?
SQUEAK SQUEAK SQUEAK SQUEAK.
SQUEAK SQUEAK SQUEAK SQUEAK SQUEAK.
DO YOU HEAR HIM, ZACHARY? WATSON IS A POET! I'VE NEVER HEARD SUCH AN ARDENT DECLARATION OF LOVE.
SQUEAK SQUEAK SQUEAK SQUEAK SQUEAK.
POOR THINGS.
LADY RITA ANSWERED HIM BACK WITH GENTLE WORDS, TOO.
YES, BUT PAINFUL AT THE SAME TIME BECAUSE, AS HE SAID, LOVE BETWEEN A LIVING CREATURE AND A GHOST IS IMPOSSIBLE.
SQUEAK.
ALL RIGHT, LADY RATINGHAM, YOU CAN GO NOW.

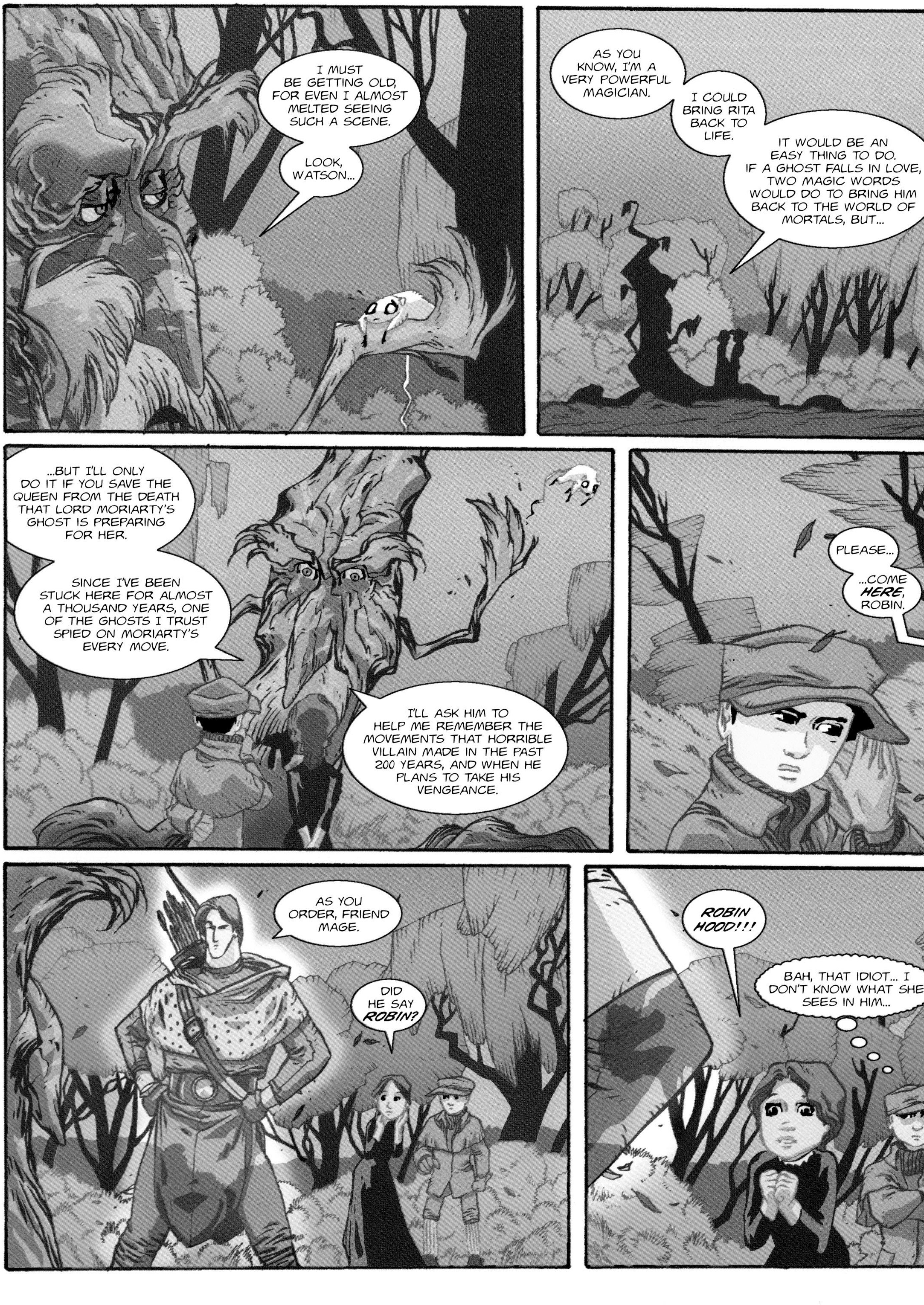
I MUST BE GETTING OLD, FOR EVEN I ALMOST MELTED SEEING SUCH A SCENE.
LOOK, WATSON...
AS YOU KNOW, I'M A VERY POWERFUL MAGICIAN.
I COULD BRING RITA BACK TO LIFE.
IT WOULD BE AN EASY THING TO DO. IF A GHOST FALLS IN LOVE, TWO MAGIC WORDS WOULD DO TO BRING HIM BACK TO THE WORLD OF MORTALS, BUT...
...BUT I'LL ONLY DO IT IF YOU SAVE THE QUEEN FROM THE DEATH THAT LORD MORIARTY'S GHOST IS PREPARING FOR HER.
SINCE I'VE BEEN STUCK HERE FOR ALMOST A THOUSAND YEARS, ONE OF THE GHOSTS I TRUST SPIED ON MORIARTY'S EVERY MOVE.
I'LL ASK HIM TO HELP ME REMEMBER THE MOVEMENTS THAT HORRIBLE VILLAIN MADE IN THE PAST 200 YEARS, AND WHEN HE PLANS TO TAKE HIS VENGEANCE.
PLEASE...
...COME HERE, ROBIN.
AS YOU ORDER, FRIEND MAGE.
DID HE SAY ROBIN?
ROBIN HOOD!!!
BAH, THAT IDIOT... I DON'T KNOW WHAT SHE SEES IN HIM...

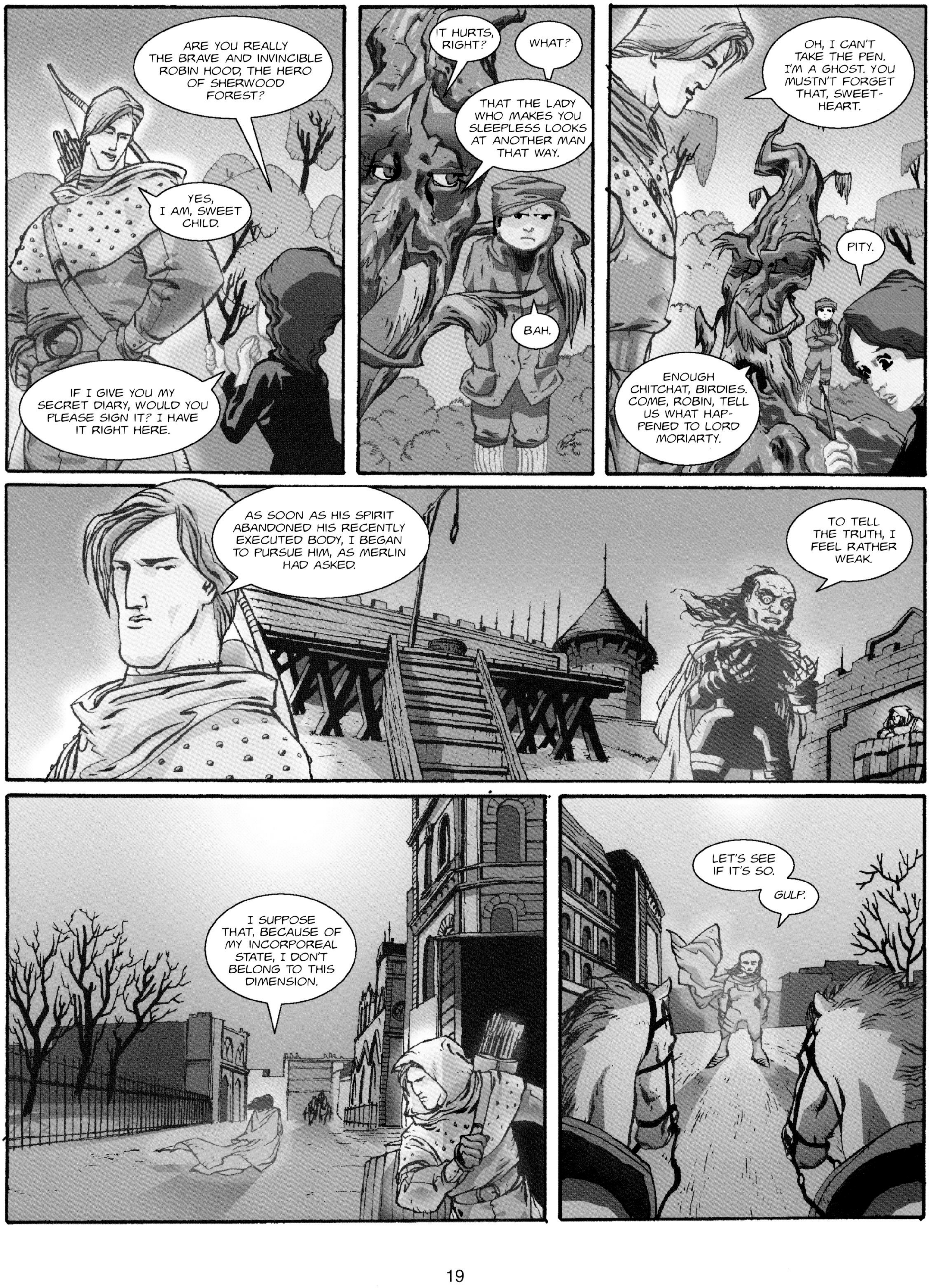
ARE YOU REALLY THE BRAVE AND INVINCIBLE ROBIN HOOD, THE HERO OF SHERWOOD FOREST?
YES, I AM, SWEET CHILD.
IF I GIVE YOU MY SECRET DIARY, WOULD YOU PLEASE SIGN IT? I HAVE IT RIGHT HERE.
IT HURTS, RIGHT?
WHAT?
THAT THE LADY WHO MAKES YOU SLEEPLESS LOOKS AT ANOTHER MAN THAT WAY.
BAH.
OH, I CAN'T TAKE THE PEN. I'M A GHOST. YOU MUSTN'T FORGET THAT, SWEET-HEART.
PITY.
ENOUGH CHITCHAT, BIRDIES. COME, ROBIN, TELL US WHAT HAP-PENED TO LORD MORIARTY.
AS SOON AS HIS SPIRIT ABANDONED HIS RECENTLY EXECUTED BODY, I BEGAN TO PURSUE HIM, AS MERLIN HAD ASKED.
TO TELL THE TRUTH, I FEEL RATHER WEAK.
I SUPPOSE THAT, BECAUSE OF MY INCORPOREAL STATE, I DON'T BELONG TO THIS DIMENSION.
LET'S SEE IF IT'S SO.
GULP.

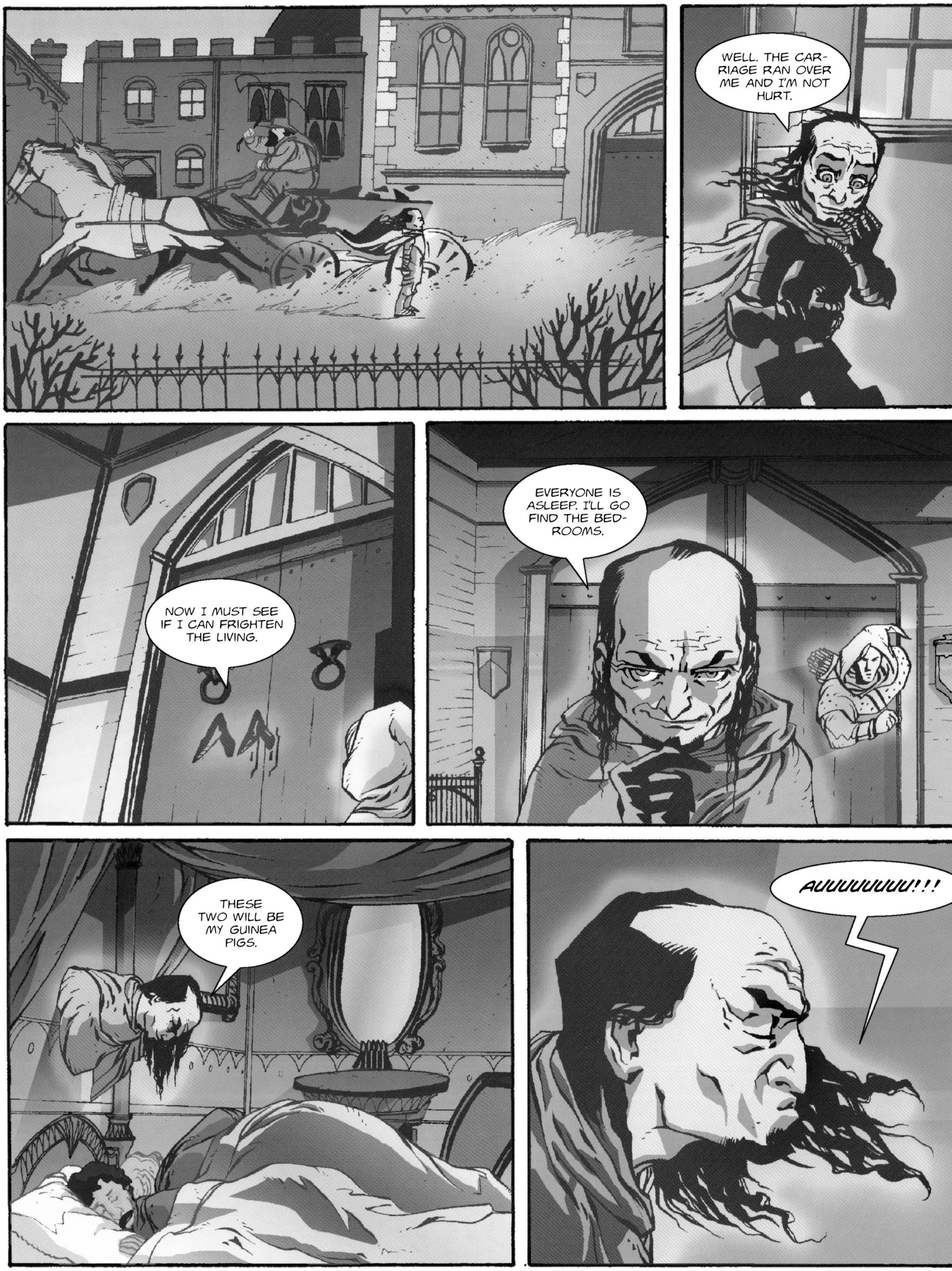
WELL. THE CARRIAGE RAN OVER ME AND I'M NOT HURT.
NOW I MUST SEE IF I CAN FRIGHTEN THE LIVING.
EVERYONE IS ASLEEP. I'LL GO FIND THE BEDROOMS.
THESE TWO WILL BE MY GUINEA PIGS.
AUUUUUUUU!!!

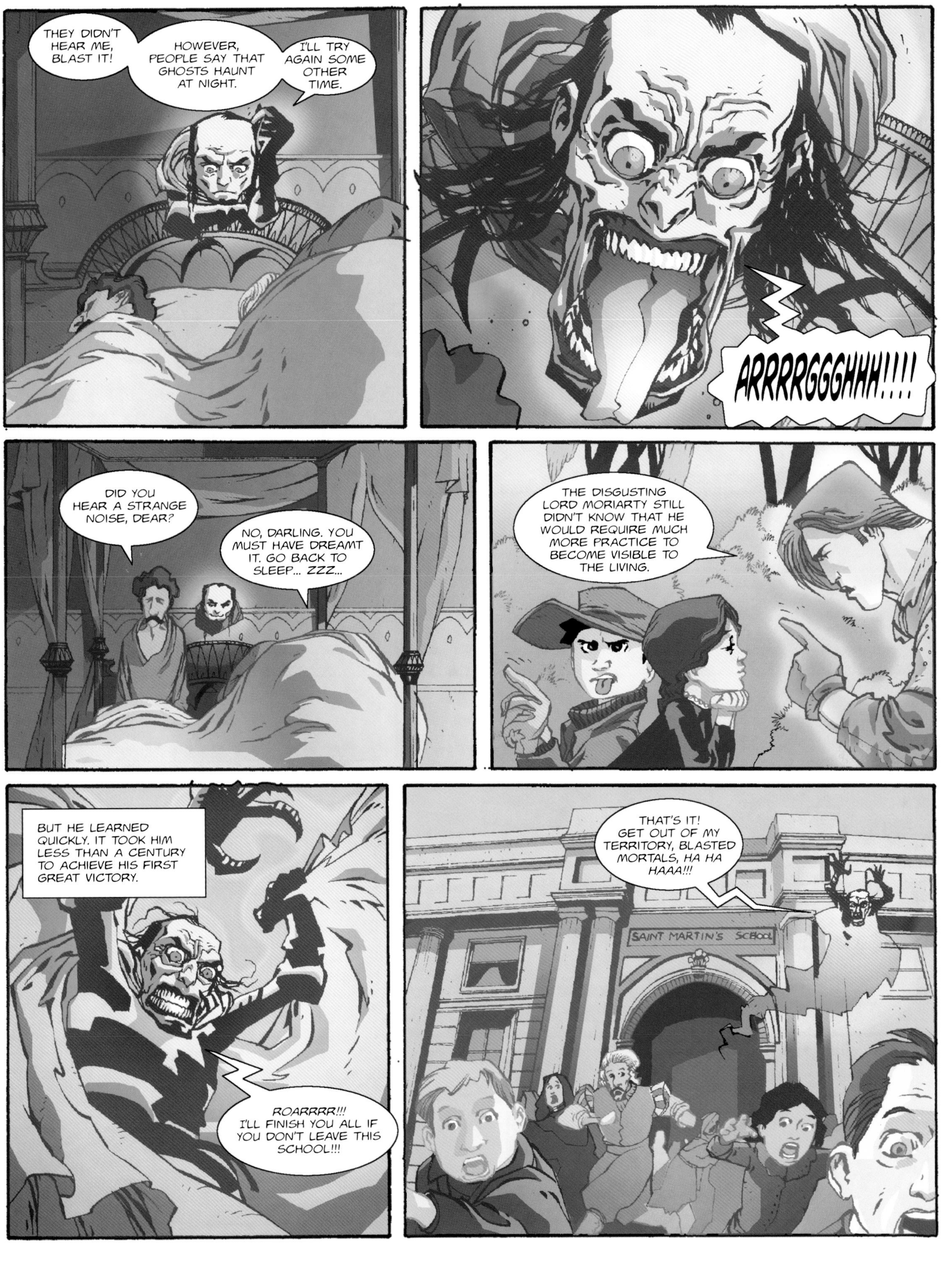
THEY DIDN'T HEAR ME, BLAST IT!
HOWEVER, PEOPLE SAY THAT GHOSTS HAUNT AT NIGHT.
I'LL TRY AGAIN SOME OTHER TIME.
ARRRRGGGHHH!!!!
DID YOU HEAR A STRANGE NOISE, DEAR?
NO, DARLING. YOU MUST HAVE DREAMT IT. GO BACK TO SLEEP... ZZZ...
THE DISGUSTING LORD MORIARTY STILL DIDN'T KNOW THAT HE WOULD REQUIRE MUCH MORE PRACTICE TO BECOME VISIBLE TO THE LIVING.
BUT HE LEARNED QUICKLY. IT TOOK HIM LESS THAN A CENTURY TO ACHIEVE HIS FIRST GREAT VICTORY.
ROARRRR!!! I'LL FINISH YOU ALL IF YOU DON'T LEAVE THIS SCHOOL!!!
THAT'S IT! GET OUT OF MY TERRITORY, BLASTED MORTALS, HA HA HAAA!!!
SAINT MARTIN'S SCHOOL

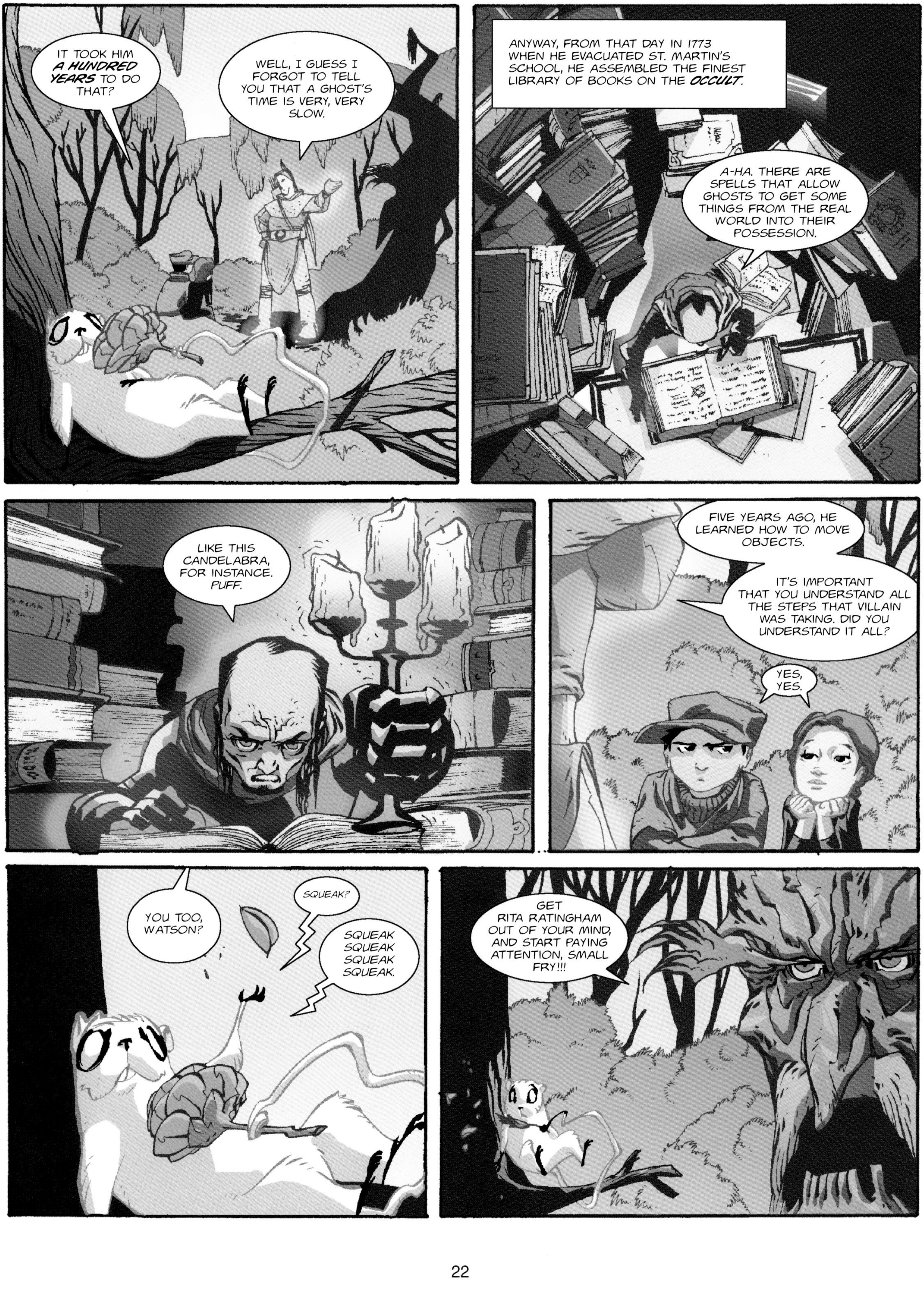
IT TOOK HIM A HUNDRED YEARS TO DO THAT?
WELL, I GUESS I FORGOT TO TELL YOU THAT A GHOST'S TIME IS VERY, VERY SLOW.
ANYWAY, FROM THAT DAY IN 1773 WHEN HE EVACUATED ST. MARTIN'S SCHOOL, HE ASSEMBLED THE FINEST LIBRARY OF BOOKS ON THE OCCULT.
A-HA. THERE ARE SPELLS THAT ALLOW GHOSTS TO GET SOME THINGS FROM THE REAL WORLD INTO THEIR POSSESSION.
LIKE THIS CANDELABRA, FOR INSTANCE. PUFF.
FIVE YEARS AGO, HE LEARNED HOW TO MOVE OBJECTS.
IT'S IMPORTANT THAT YOU UNDERSTAND ALL THE STEPS THAT VILLAIN WAS TAKING. DID YOU UNDERSTAND IT ALL?
YES, YES.
YOU TOO, WATSON?
SQUEAK?
SQUEAK SQUEAK SQUEAK SQUEAK.
GET RITA RATINGHAM OUT OF YOUR MIND, AND START PAYING ATTENTION, SMALL FRY!!!

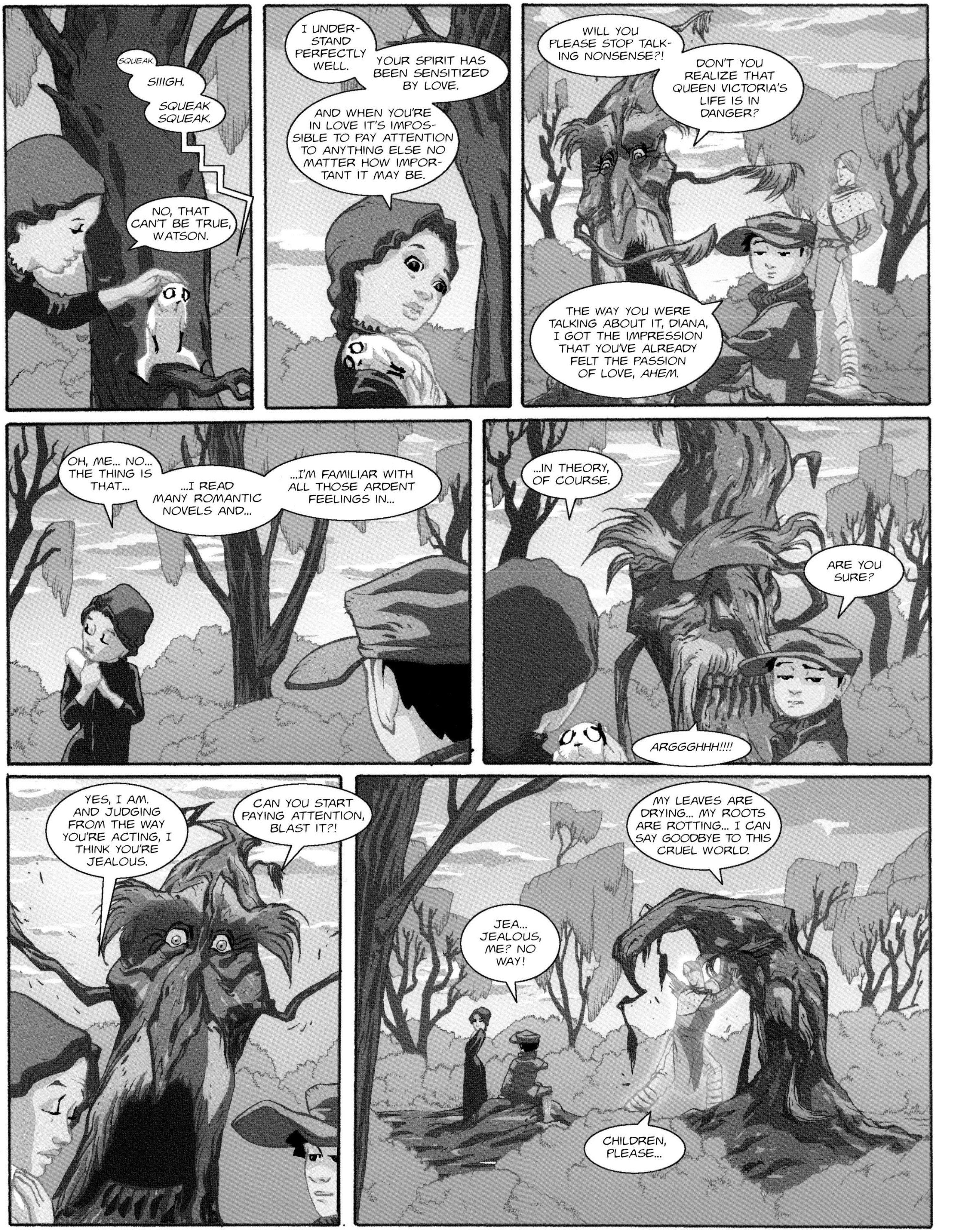
SQUEAK.
SIIIGH.
SQUEAK SQUEAK.
NO, THAT CAN'T BE TRUE, WATSON.
I UNDERSTAND PERFECTLY WELL.
YOUR SPIRIT HAS BEEN SENSITIZED BY LOVE.
AND WHEN YOU'RE IN LOVE IT'S IMPOSSIBLE TO PAY ATTENTION TO ANYTHING ELSE NO MATTER HOW IMPORTANT IT MAY BE.
WILL YOU PLEASE STOP TALKING NONSENSE?!
DON'T YOU REALIZE THAT QUEEN VICTORIA'S LIFE IS IN DANGER?
THE WAY YOU WERE TALKING ABOUT IT, DIANA, I GOT THE IMPRESSION THAT YOU'VE ALREADY FELT THE PASSION OF LOVE, AHEM.
OH, ME... NO... THE THING IS THAT...
...I READ MANY ROMANTIC NOVELS AND...
...I'M FAMILIAR WITH ALL THOSE ARDENT FEELINGS IN...
...IN THEORY, OF COURSE.
ARE YOU SURE?
ARGGGHHH!!!!
YES, I AM. AND JUDGING FROM THE WAY YOU'RE ACTING, I THINK YOU'RE JEALOUS.
CAN YOU START PAYING ATTENTION, BLAST IT?!
MY LEAVES ARE DRYING... MY ROOTS ARE ROTTING... I CAN SAY GOODBYE TO THIS CRUEL WORLD.
JEA... JEALOUS, ME? NO WAY!
CHILDREN, PLEASE...

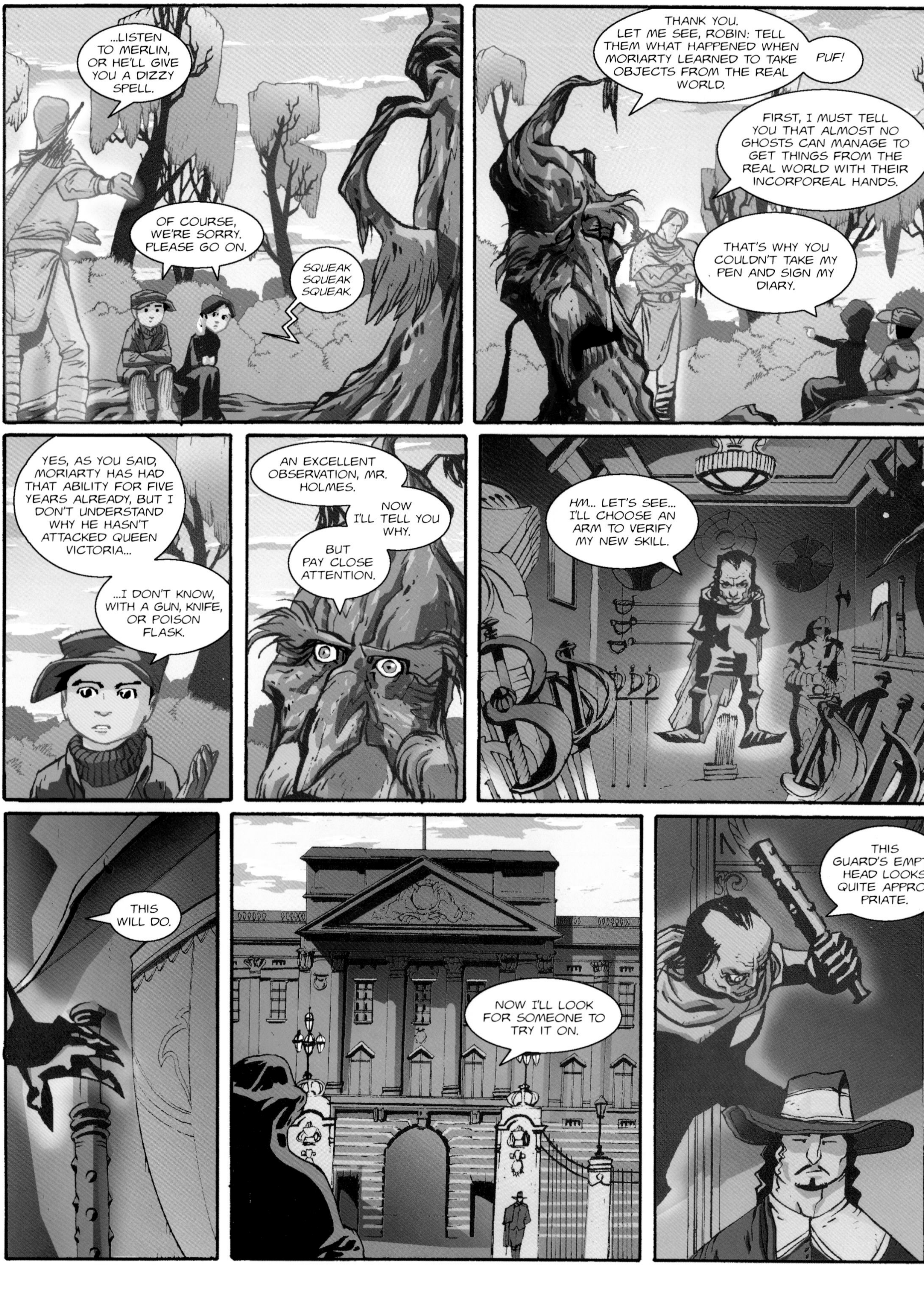
...LISTEN TO MERLIN, OR HE'LL GIVE YOU A DIZZY SPELL.
OF COURSE, WE'RE SORRY. PLEASE GO ON.
SQUEAK SQUEAK SQUEAK.
THANK YOU. LET ME SEE, ROBIN: TELL THEM WHAT HAPPENED WHEN MORIARTY LEARNED TO TAKE OBJECTS FROM THE REAL WORLD.
PUF!
FIRST, I MUST TELL YOU THAT ALMOST NO GHOSTS CAN MANAGE TO GET THINGS FROM THE REAL WORLD WITH THEIR INCORPOREAL HANDS.
THAT'S WHY YOU COULDN'T TAKE MY PEN AND SIGN MY DIARY.
YES, AS YOU SAID, MORIARTY HAS HAD THAT ABILITY FOR FIVE YEARS ALREADY, BUT I DON'T UNDERSTAND WHY HE HASN'T ATTACKED QUEEN VICTORIA...
...I DON'T KNOW, WITH A GUN, KNIFE, OR POISON FLASK.
AN EXCELLENT OBSERVATION, MR. HOLMES.
NOW I'LL TELL YOU WHY.
BUT PAY CLOSE ATTENTION.
HM... LET'S SEE... I'LL CHOOSE AN ARM TO VERIFY MY NEW SKILL.
THIS WILL DO.
NOW I'LL LOOK FOR SOMEONE TO TRY IT ON.
THIS GUARD'S EMPTY HEAD LOOKS QUITE APPRO-PRIATE.

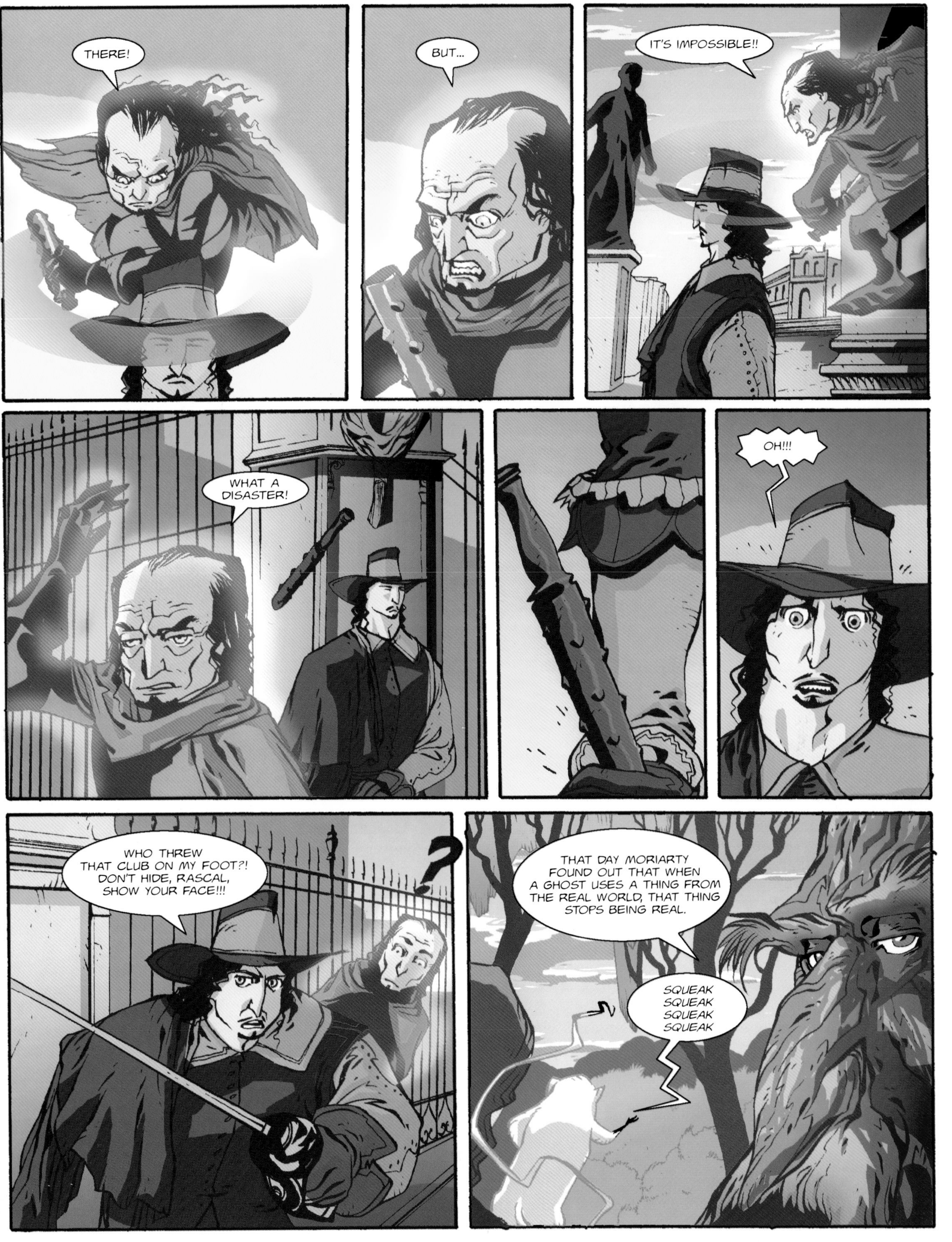
THERE!
BUT...
IT'S IMPOSSIBLE!!
WHAT A DISASTER!
OH!!!
WHO THREW THAT CLUB ON MY FOOT?! DON'T HIDE, RASCAL, SHOW YOUR FACE!!!
THAT DAY MORIARTY FOUND OUT THAT WHEN A GHOST USES A THING FROM THE REAL WORLD, THAT THING STOPS BEING REAL.
SQUEAK SQUEAK SQUEAK SQUEAK

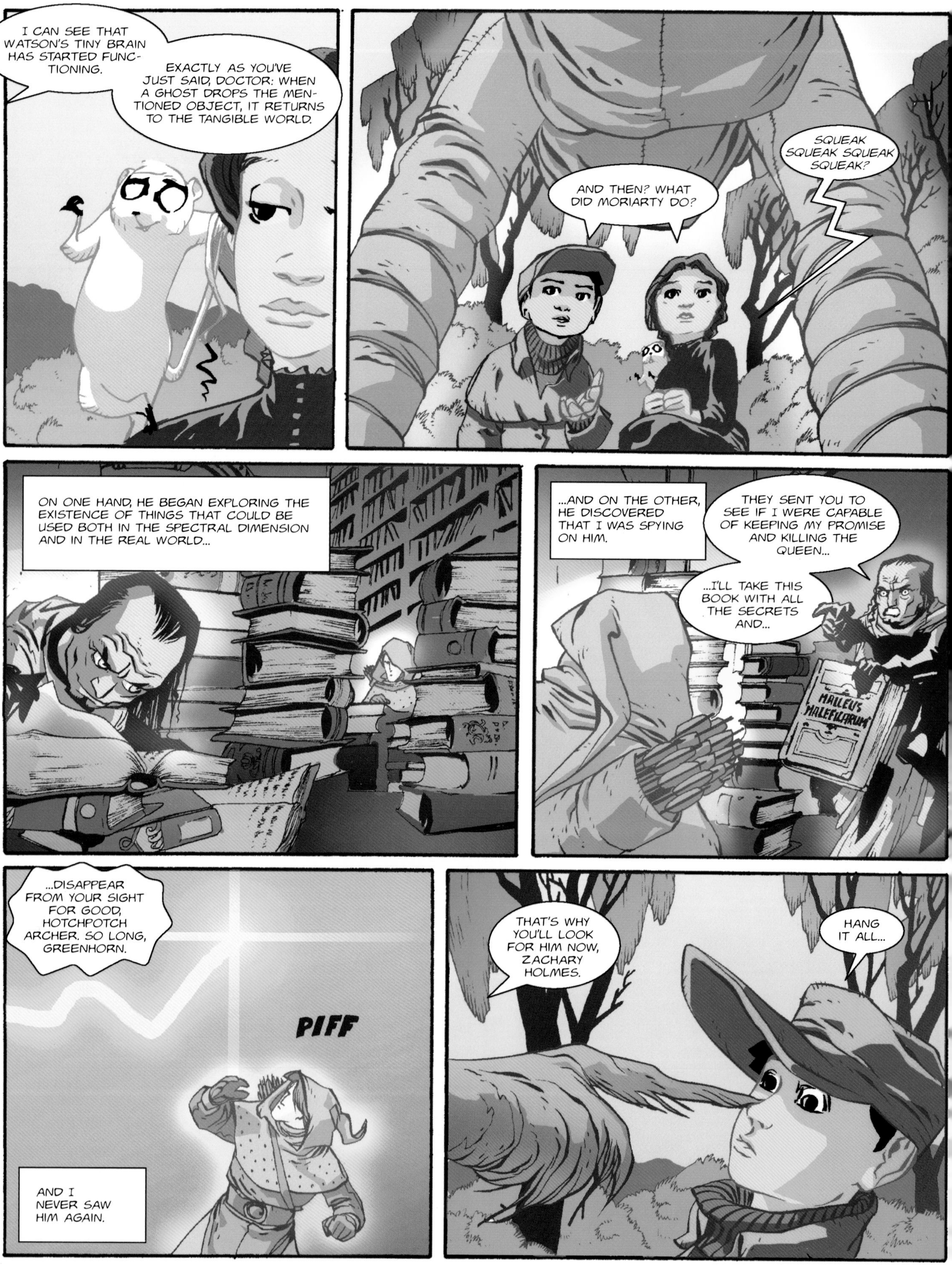
I CAN SEE THAT WATSON'S TINY BRAIN HAS STARTED FUNCTIONING.
EXACTLY AS YOU'VE JUST SAID, DOCTOR: WHEN A GHOST DROPS THE MENTIONED OBJECT, IT RETURNS TO THE TANGIBLE WORLD.
AND THEN? WHAT DID MORIARTY DO?
SQUEAK SQUEAK SQUEAK SQUEAK?
ON ONE HAND, HE BEGAN EXPLORING THE EXISTENCE OF THINGS THAT COULD BE USED BOTH IN THE SPECTRAL DIMENSION AND IN THE REAL WORLD...
...AND ON THE OTHER, HE DISCOVERED THAT I WAS SPYING ON HIM.
THEY SENT YOU TO SEE IF I WERE CAPABLE OF KEEPING MY PROMISE AND KILLING THE QUEEN...
...I'LL TAKE THIS BOOK WITH ALL THE SECRETS AND...
MALLEUS MALEFICARUM
...DISAPPEAR FROM YOUR SIGHT FOR GOOD, HOTCHPOTCH ARCHER. SO LONG, GREENHORN.
PIFF
AND I NEVER SAW HIM AGAIN.
THAT'S WHY YOU'LL LOOK FOR HIM NOW, ZACHARY HOLMES.
HANG IT ALL...

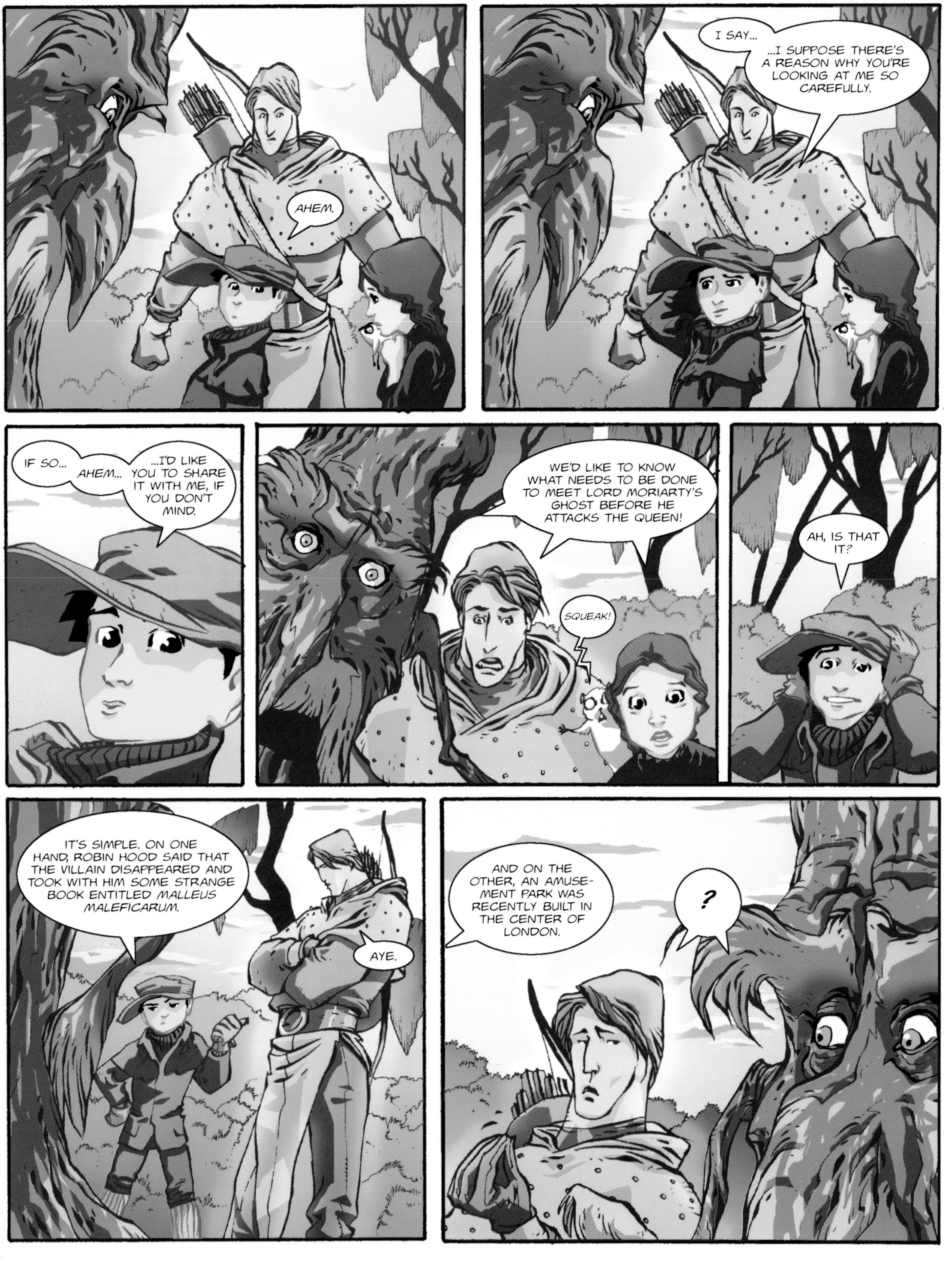
AHEM.
I SAY...
...I SUPPOSE THERE'S A REASON WHY YOU'RE LOOKING AT ME SO CAREFULLY.
IF SO...
AHEM...
...I'D LIKE YOU TO SHARE IT WITH ME, IF YOU DON'T MIND.
WE'D LIKE TO KNOW WHAT NEEDS TO BE DONE TO MEET LORD MORIARTY'S GHOST BEFORE HE ATTACKS THE QUEEN!
SQUEAK!
AH, IS THAT IT?
IT'S SIMPLE. ON ONE HAND, ROBIN HOOD SAID THAT THE VILLAIN DISAPPEARED AND TOOK WITH HIM SOME STRANGE BOOK ENTITLED MALLEUS MALEFICARUM.
AYE.
AND ON THE OTHER, AN AMUSE-MENT PARK WAS RECENTLY BUILT IN THE CENTER OF LONDON.
?

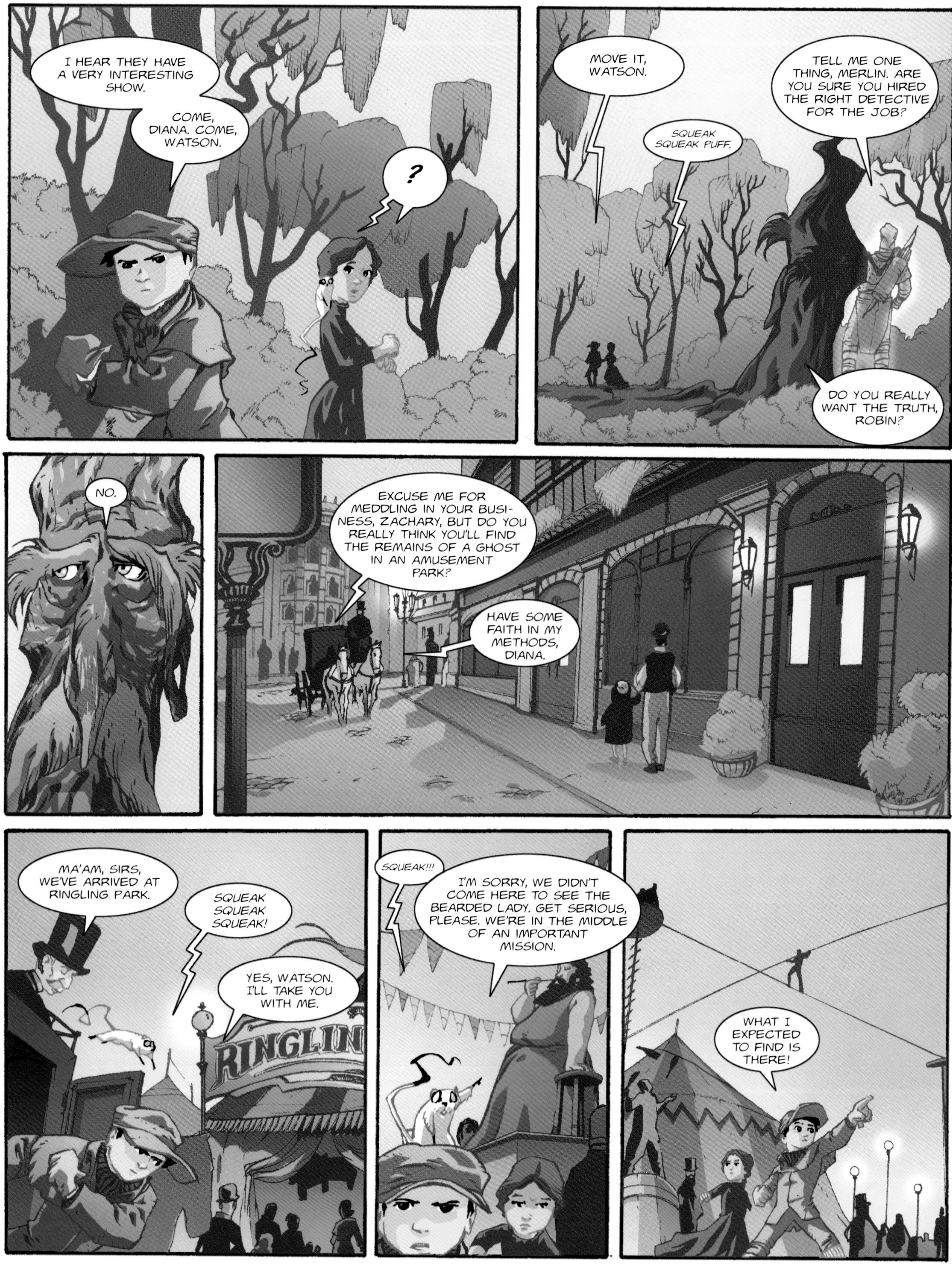
I HEAR THEY HAVE A VERY INTERESTING SHOW.
COME, DIANA. COME, WATSON.
?
MOVE IT, WATSON.
SQUEAK SQUEAK PUFF.
TELL ME ONE THING, MERLIN. ARE YOU SURE YOU HIRED THE RIGHT DETECTIVE FOR THE JOB?
DO YOU REALLY WANT THE TRUTH, ROBIN?
NO.
EXCUSE ME FOR MEDDLING IN YOUR BUSINESS, ZACHARY, BUT DO YOU REALLY THINK YOU'LL FIND THE REMAINS OF A GHOST IN AN AMUSEMENT PARK?
HAVE SOME FAITH IN MY METHODS, DIANA.
MA'AM, SIRS, WE'VE ARRIVED AT RINGLING PARK.
SQUEAK SQUEAK SQUEAK!
YES, WATSON. I'LL TAKE YOU WITH ME.
RINGLIN
SQUEAK!!!
I'M SORRY, WE DIDN'T COME HERE TO SEE THE BEARDED LADY. GET SERIOUS, PLEASE. WE'RE IN THE MIDDLE OF AN IMPORTANT MISSION.
WHAT I EXPECTED TO FIND IS THERE!

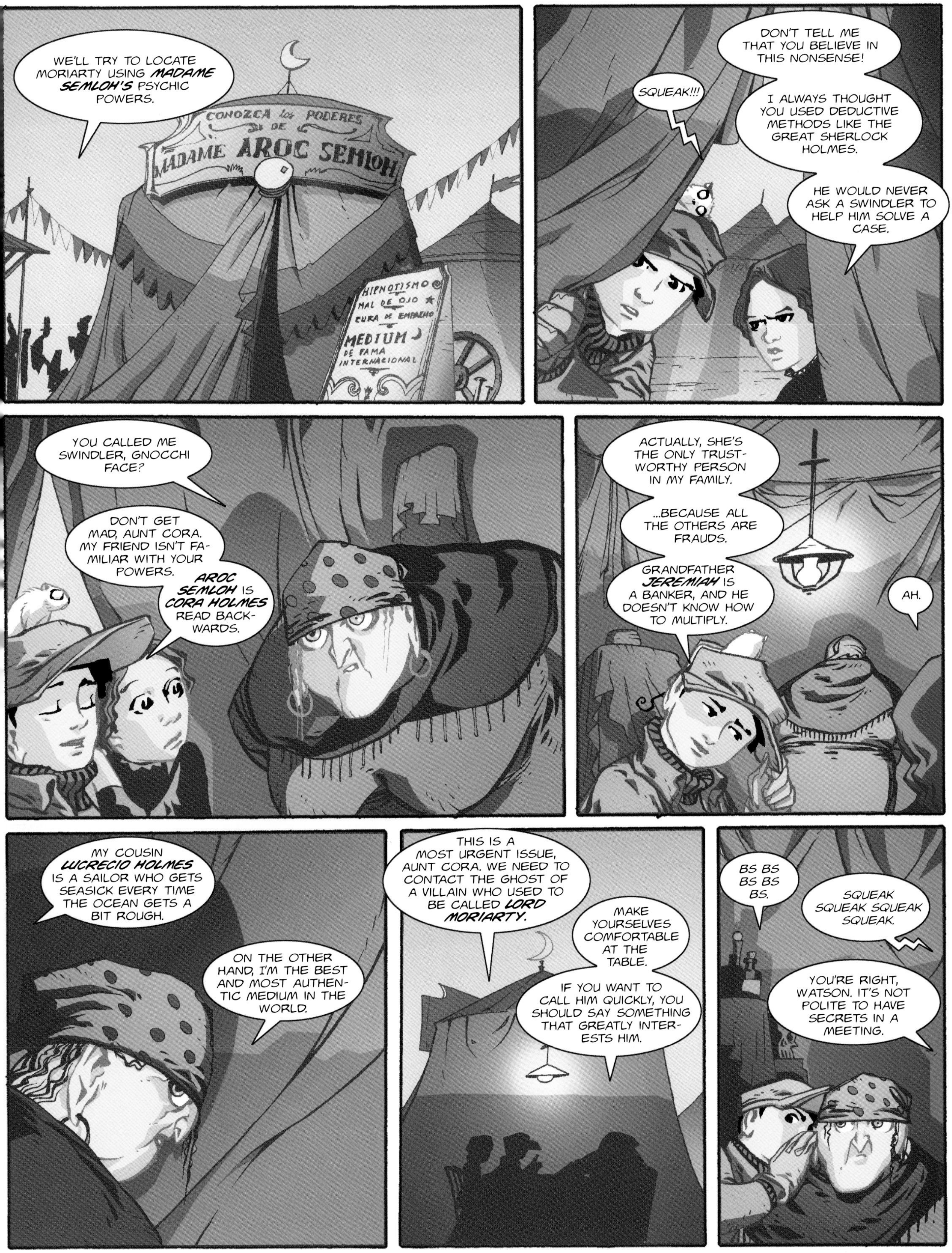

WE'LL TRY TO LOCATE MORIARTY USING MADAME SEMLOH'S PSYCHIC POWERS.
CONOZCA los PODERES DE MADAME AROC SEMLOH
HIPNOTISMO MAL DE OJO CURA DE EMPACHO MEDIUM DE FAMA INTERNACIONAL
SQUEAK!!!
DON'T TELL ME THAT YOU BELIEVE IN THIS NONSENSE!
I ALWAYS THOUGHT YOU USED DEDUCTIVE METHODS LIKE THE GREAT SHERLOCK HOLMES.
HE WOULD NEVER ASK A SWINDLER TO HELP HIM SOLVE A CASE.
YOU CALLED ME SWINDLER, GNOCCHI FACE?
DON'T GET MAD, AUNT CORA. MY FRIEND ISN'T FAMILIAR WITH YOUR POWERS.
AROC SEMLOH IS CORA HOLMES READ BACKWARDS.
ACTUALLY, SHE'S THE ONLY TRUSTWORTHY PERSON IN MY FAMILY.
...BECAUSE ALL THE OTHERS ARE FRAUDS.
GRANDFATHER JEREMIAH IS A BANKER, AND HE DOESN'T KNOW HOW TO MULTIPLY.
AH.
MY COUSIN LUCRECIO HOLMES IS A SAILOR WHO GETS SEASICK EVERY TIME THE OCEAN GETS A BIT ROUGH.
ON THE OTHER HAND, I'M THE BEST AND MOST AUTHENTIC MEDIUM IN THE WORLD.
THIS IS A MOST URGENT ISSUE, AUNT CORA. WE NEED TO CONTACT THE GHOST OF A VILLAIN WHO USED TO BE CALLED LORD MORIARTY.
MAKE YOURSELVES COMFORTABLE AT THE TABLE.
IF YOU WANT TO CALL HIM QUICKLY, YOU SHOULD SAY SOMETHING THAT GREATLY INTERESTS HIM.
BS BS BS BS BS.
SQUEAK SQUEAK SQUEAK SQUEAK.
YOU'RE RIGHT, WATSON. IT'S NOT POLITE TO HAVE SECRETS IN A MEETING.

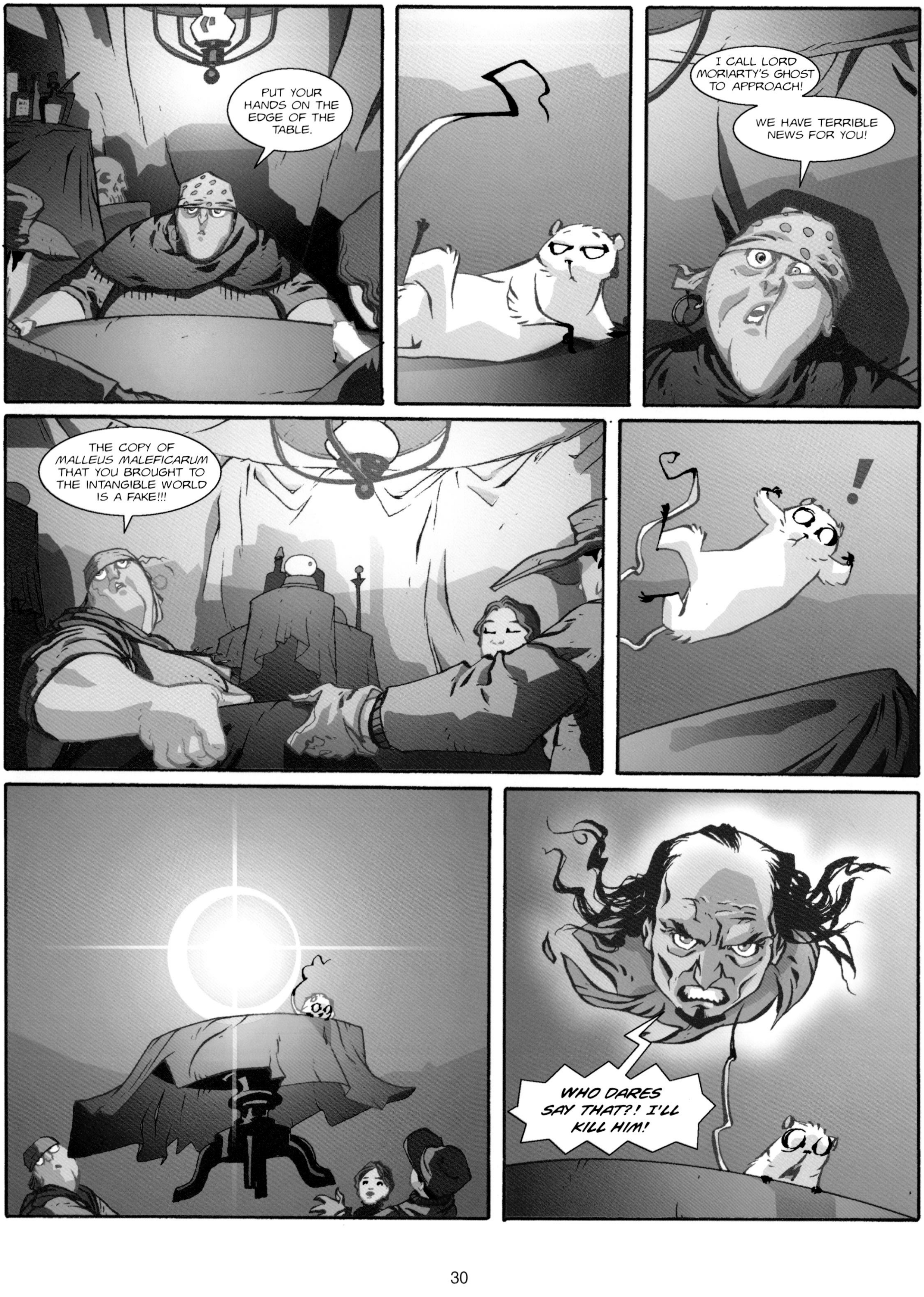
PUT YOUR HANDS ON THE EDGE OF THE TABLE.
I CALL LORD MORIARTY'S GHOST TO APPROACH!
WE HAVE TERRIBLE NEWS FOR YOU!
THE COPY OF MALLEUS MALEFICARUM THAT YOU BROUGHT TO THE INTANGIBLE WORLD IS A FAKE!!!
!
WHO DARES SAY THAT?! I'LL KILL HIM!

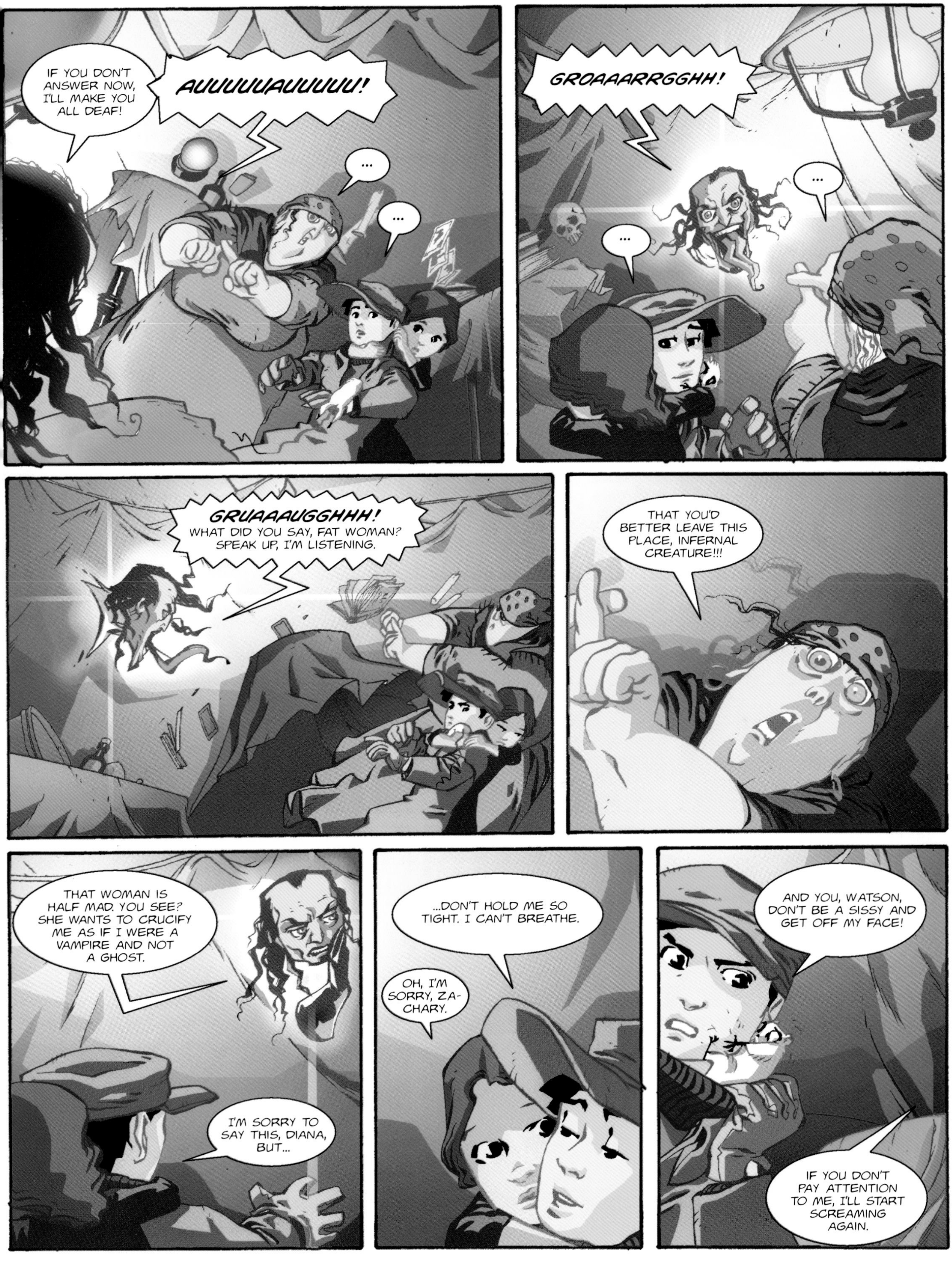
IF YOU DON'T ANSWER NOW, I'LL MAKE YOU ALL DEAF!
AUUUUUAUUUUU!
...
...
GROAAARRGGHH!
...
...
GRUAAAUGGHHH! WHAT DID YOU SAY, FAT WOMAN? SPEAK UP, I'M LISTENING.
THAT YOU'D BETTER LEAVE THIS PLACE, INFERNAL CREATURE!!!
THAT WOMAN IS HALF MAD. YOU SEE? SHE WANTS TO CRUCIFY ME AS IF I WERE A VAMPIRE AND NOT A GHOST.
I'M SORRY TO SAY THIS, DIANA, BUT...
...DON'T HOLD ME SO TIGHT. I CAN'T BREATHE.
OH, I'M SORRY, ZA-CHARY.
AND YOU, WATSON, DON'T BE A SISSY AND GET OFF MY FACE!
IF YOU DON'T PAY ATTENTION TO ME, I'LL START SCREAMING AGAIN.

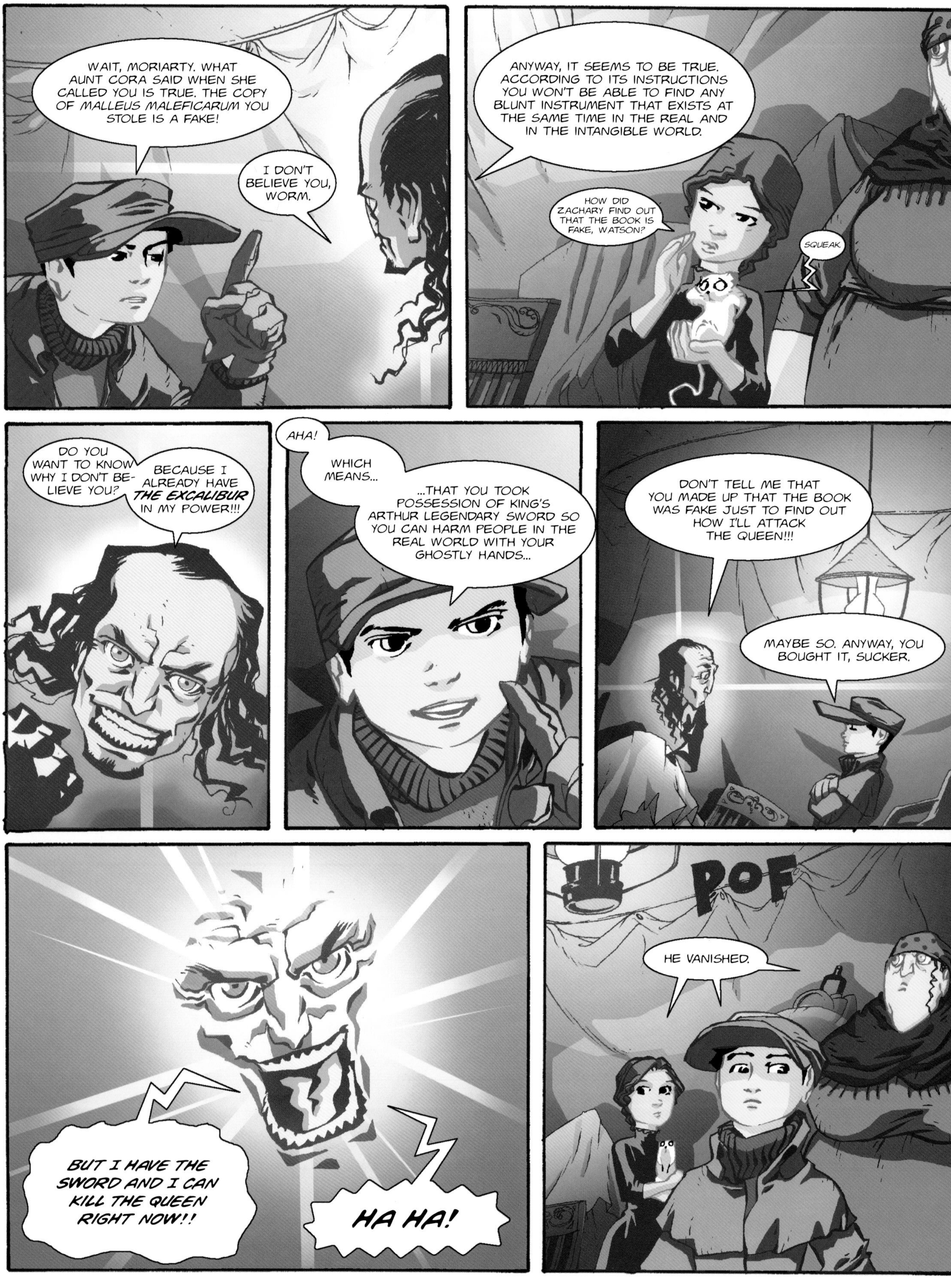
WAIT, MORIARTY. WHAT AUNT CORA SAID WHEN SHE CALLED YOU IS TRUE. THE COPY OF MALLEUS MALEFICARUM YOU STOLE IS A FAKE!
I DON'T BELIEVE YOU, WORM.
ANYWAY, IT SEEMS TO BE TRUE. ACCORDING TO ITS INSTRUCTIONS YOU WON'T BE ABLE TO FIND ANY BLUNT INSTRUMENT THAT EXISTS AT THE SAME TIME IN THE REAL AND IN THE INTANGIBLE WORLD.
HOW DID ZACHARY FIND OUT THAT THE BOOK IS FAKE, WATSON?
SQUEAK.
DO YOU WANT TO KNOW WHY I DON'T BE-LIEVE YOU?
BECAUSE I ALREADY HAVE THE EXCALIBUR IN MY POWER!!!
AHA!
WHICH MEANS...
...THAT YOU TOOK POSSESSION OF KING'S ARTHUR LEGENDARY SWORD SO YOU CAN HARM PEOPLE IN THE REAL WORLD WITH YOUR GHOSTLY HANDS...
DON'T TELL ME THAT YOU MADE UP THAT THE BOOK WAS FAKE JUST TO FIND OUT HOW I'LL ATTACK THE QUEEN!!!
MAYBE SO. ANYWAY, YOU BOUGHT IT, SUCKER.
BUT I HAVE THE SWORD AND I CAN KILL THE QUEEN RIGHT NOW!!
HA HA!
POF
HE VANISHED.

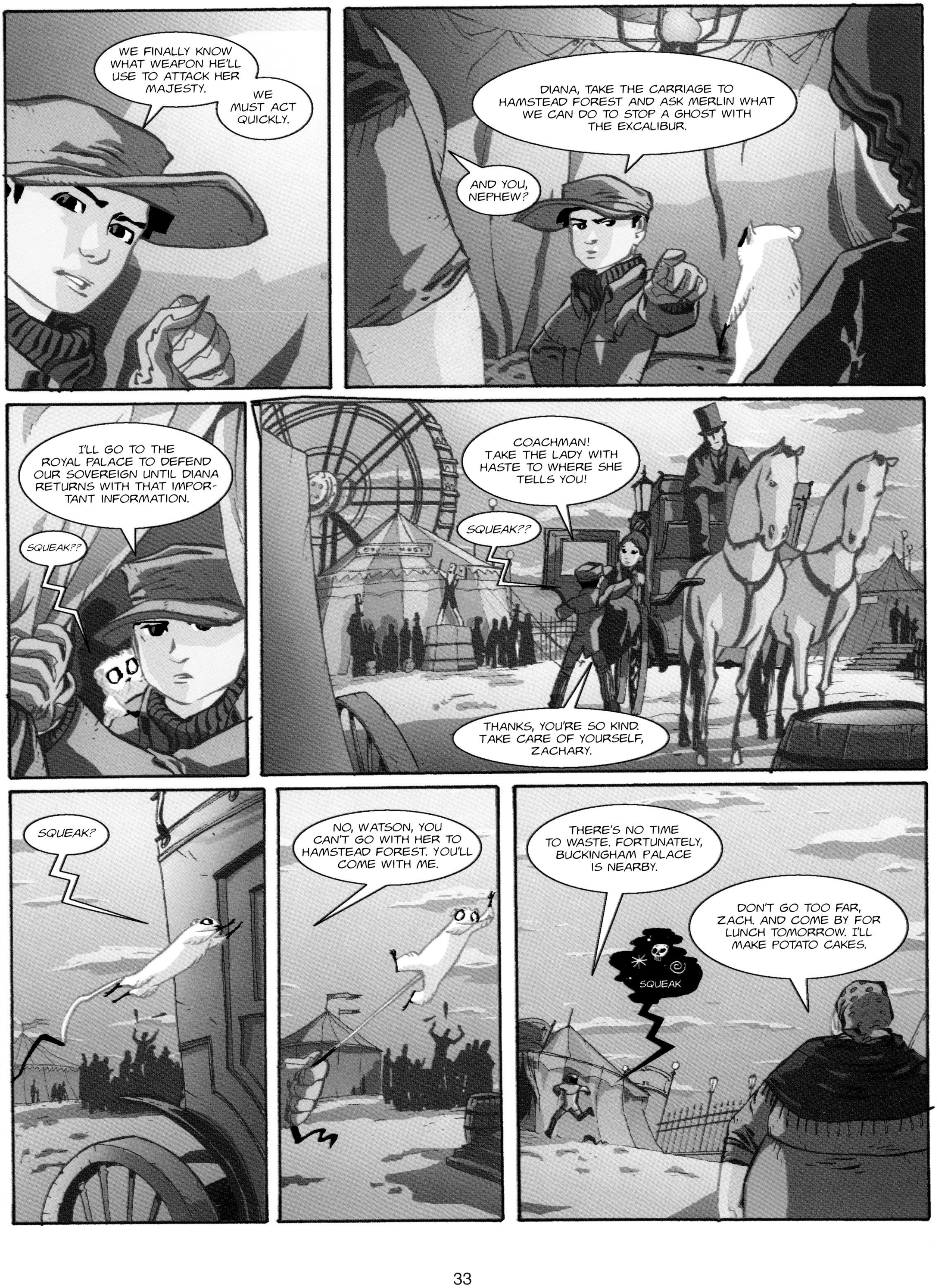
WE FINALLY KNOW WHAT WEAPON HE'LL USE TO ATTACK HER MAJESTY.
WE MUST ACT QUICKLY.
DIANA, TAKE THE CARRIAGE TO HAMSTEAD FOREST AND ASK MERLIN WHAT WE CAN DO TO STOP A GHOST WITH THE EXCALIBUR.
AND YOU, NEPHEW?
I'LL GO TO THE ROYAL PALACE TO DEFEND OUR SOVEREIGN UNTIL DIANA RETURNS WITH THAT IMPORTANT INFORMATION.
SQUEAK??
COACHMAN! TAKE THE LADY WITH HASTE TO WHERE SHE TELLS YOU!
SQUEAK??
THANKS, YOU'RE SO KIND. TAKE CARE OF YOURSELF, ZACHARY.
SQUEAK?
NO, WATSON, YOU CAN'T GO WITH HER TO HAMSTEAD FOREST. YOU'LL COME WITH ME.
THERE'S NO TIME TO WASTE. FORTUNATELY, BUCKINGHAM PALACE IS NEARBY.
SQUEAK
DON'T GO TOO FAR, ZACH. AND COME BY FOR LUNCH TOMORROW. I'LL MAKE POTATO CAKES.

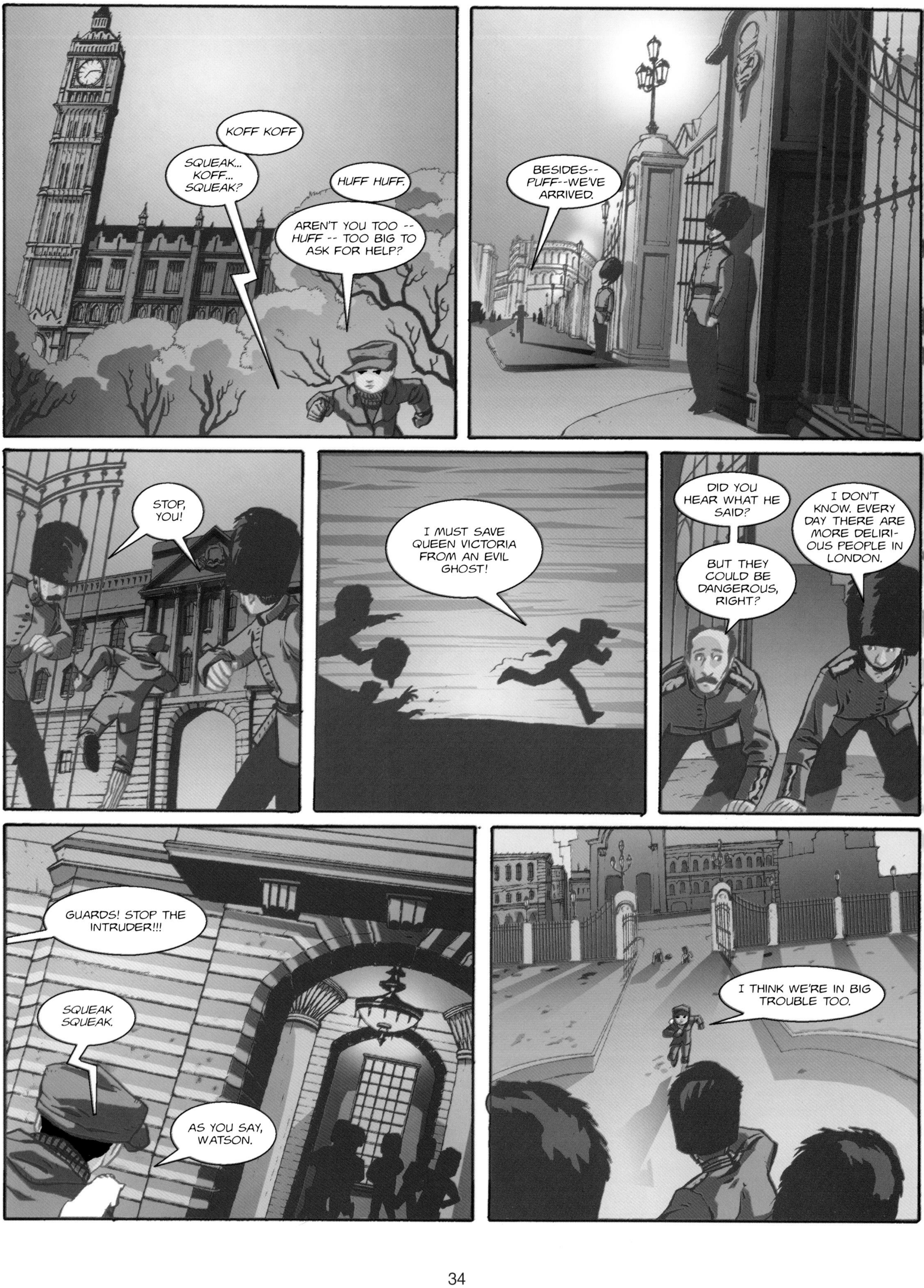
KOFF KOFF
SQUEAK... KOFF... SQUEAK?
HUFF HUFF.
AREN'T YOU TOO -- HUFF -- TOO BIG TO ASK FOR HELP?
BESIDES-- PUFF--WE'VE ARRIVED.
STOP, YOU!
I MUST SAVE QUEEN VICTORIA FROM AN EVIL GHOST!
DID YOU HEAR WHAT HE SAID?
BUT THEY COULD BE DANGEROUS, RIGHT?
I DON'T KNOW. EVERY DAY THERE ARE MORE DELIRI-OUS PEOPLE IN LONDON.
GUARDS! STOP THE INTRUDER!!!
SQUEAK SQUEAK.
AS YOU SAY, WATSON.
I THINK WE'RE IN BIG TROUBLE TOO.

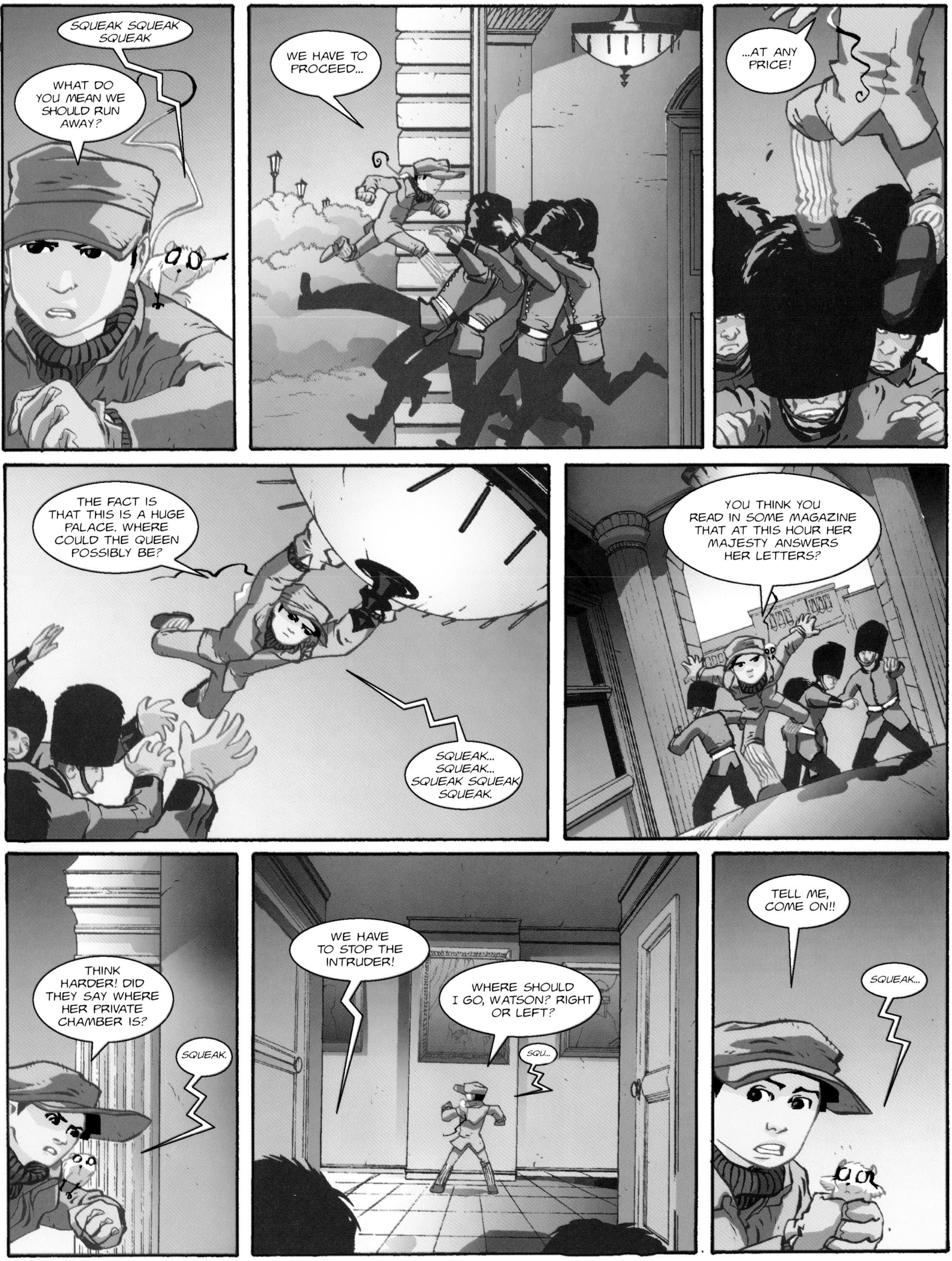

SQUEAK SQUEAK SQUEAK
WHAT DO YOU MEAN WE SHOULD RUN AWAY?
WE HAVE TO PROCEED...
...AT ANY PRICE!
THE FACT IS THAT THIS IS A HUGE PALACE. WHERE COULD THE QUEEN POSSIBLY BE?
SQUEAK... SQUEAK... SQUEAK SQUEAK SQUEAK.
YOU THINK YOU READ IN SOME MAGAZINE THAT AT THIS HOUR HER MAJESTY ANSWERS HER LETTERS?
THINK HARDER! DID THEY SAY WHERE HER PRIVATE CHAMBER IS?
SQUEAK.
WE HAVE TO STOP THE INTRUDER!
WHERE SHOULD I GO, WATSON? RIGHT OR LEFT?
SQU...
TELL ME, COME ON!!
SQUEAK...

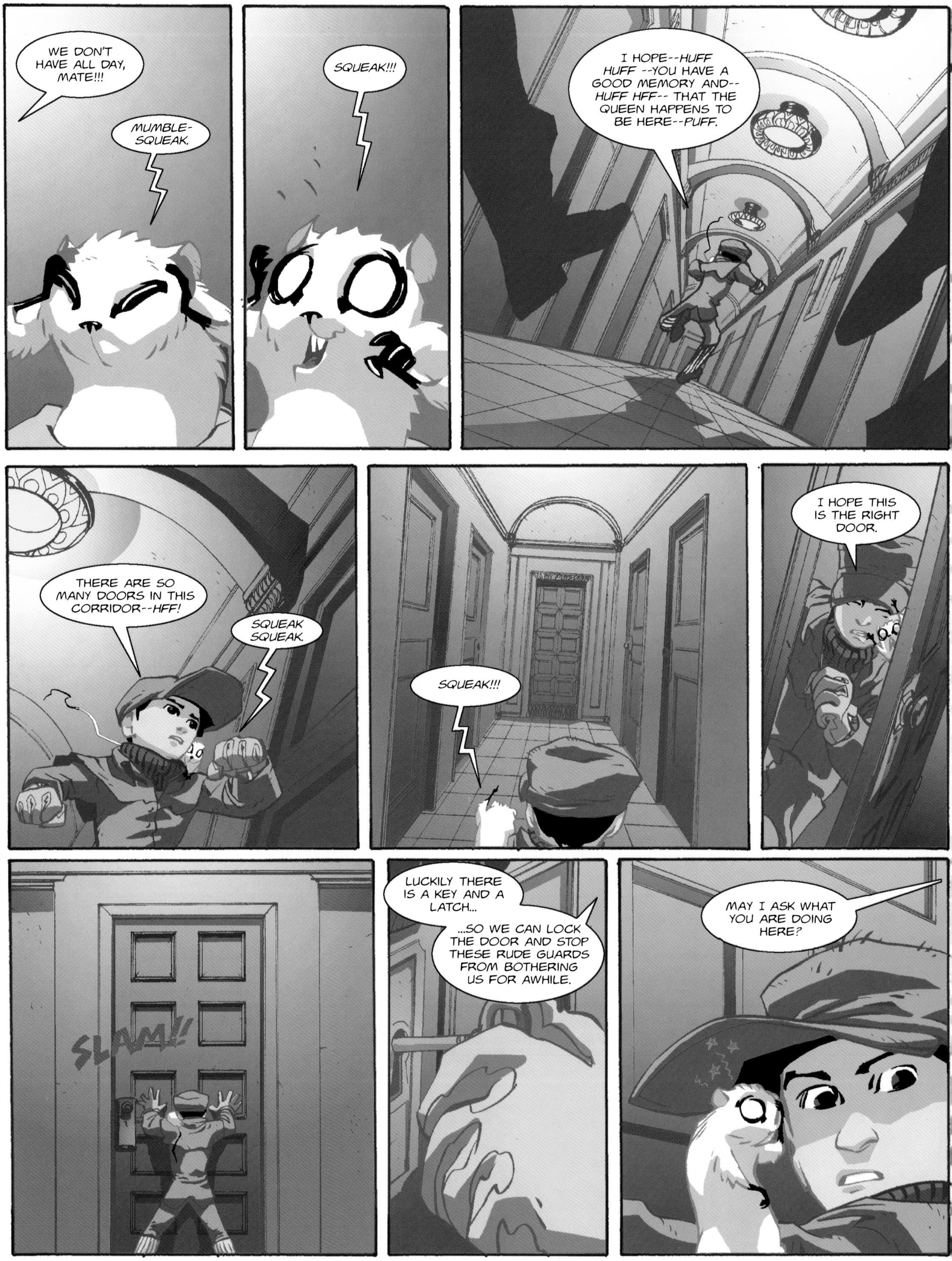
WE DON'T HAVE ALL DAY, MATE!!!
MUMBLE-SQUEAK.
SQUEAK!!!
I HOPE--HUFF HUFF --YOU HAVE A GOOD MEMORY AND--HUFF HFF-- THAT THE QUEEN HAPPENS TO BE HERE--PUFF.
THERE ARE SO MANY DOORS IN THIS CORRIDOR--HFF!
SQUEAK SQUEAK.
SQUEAK!!!
I HOPE THIS IS THE RIGHT DOOR.
SLAM!!
LUCKILY THERE IS A KEY AND A LATCH...
...SO WE CAN LOCK THE DOOR AND STOP THESE RUDE GUARDS FROM BOTHERING US FOR AWHILE.
MAY I ASK WHAT YOU ARE DOING HERE?

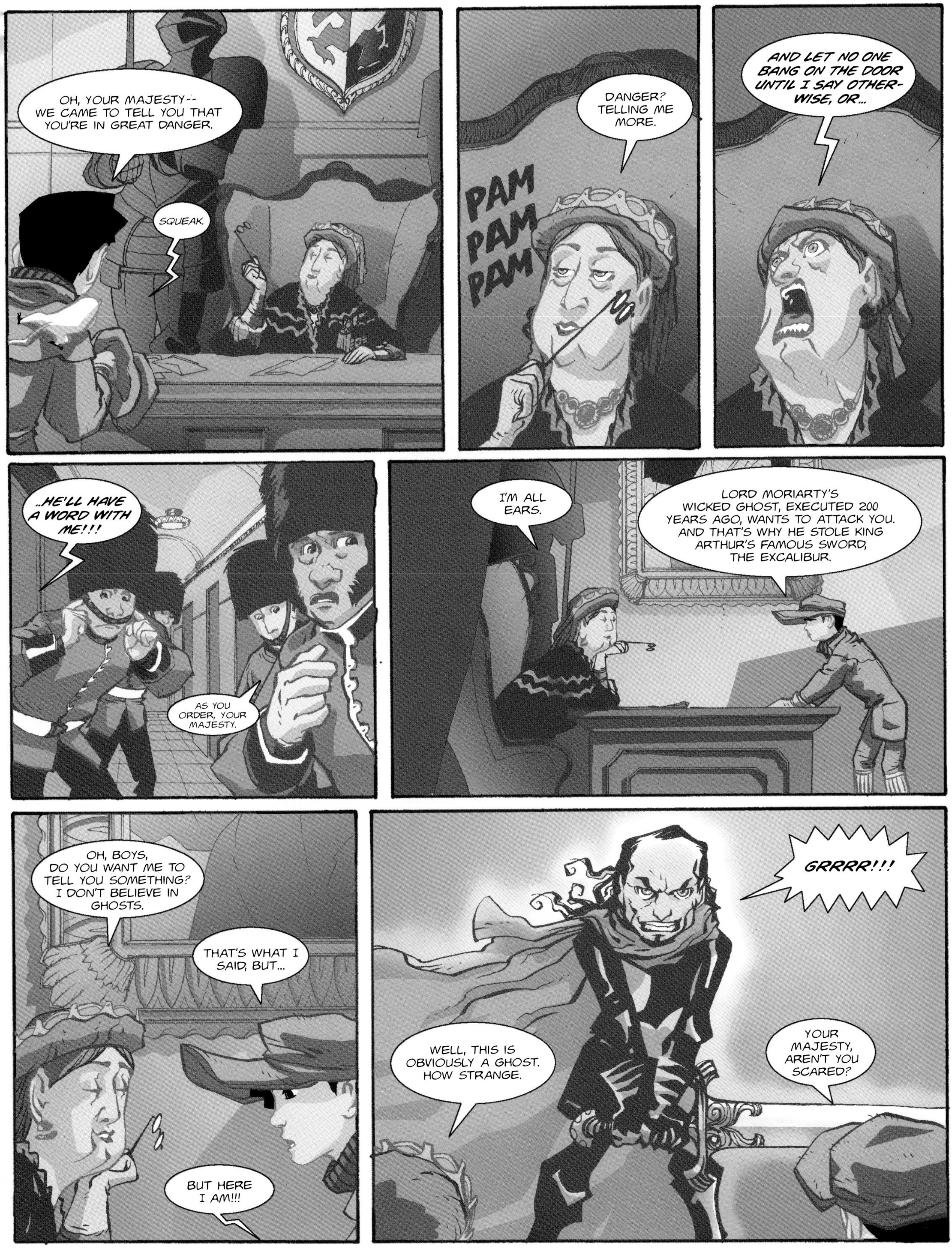
OH, YOUR MAJESTY-- WE CAME TO TELL YOU THAT YOU'RE IN GREAT DANGER.
SQUEAK.
DANGER? TELLING ME MORE.
PAM PAM PAM
AND LET NO ONE BANG ON THE DOOR UNTIL I SAY OTHER-WISE, OR...
..HE'LL HAVE A WORD WITH ME!!!
AS YOU ORDER, YOUR MAJESTY.
I'M ALL EARS.
LORD MORIARTY'S WICKED GHOST, EXECUTED 200 YEARS AGO, WANTS TO ATTACK YOU. AND THAT'S WHY HE STOLE KING ARTHUR'S FAMOUS SWORD, THE EXCALIBUR.
OH, BOYS, DO YOU WANT ME TO TELL YOU SOMETHING? I DON'T BELIEVE IN GHOSTS.
THAT'S WHAT I SAID, BUT...
BUT HERE I AM!!!
GRRRR!!!
WELL, THIS IS OBVIOUSLY A GHOST. HOW STRANGE.
YOUR MAJESTY, AREN'T YOU SCARED?

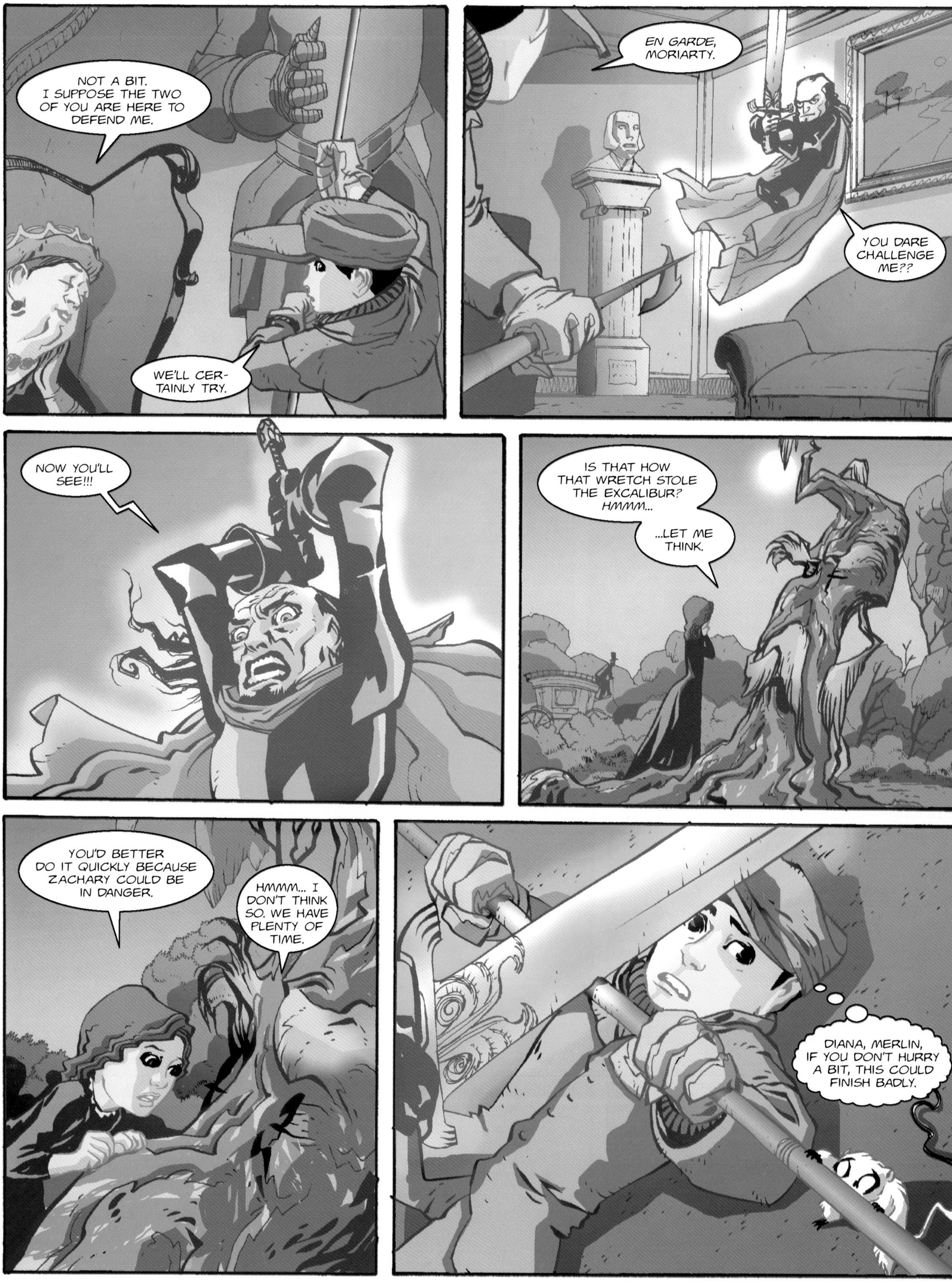
NOT A BIT. I SUPPOSE THE TWO OF YOU ARE HERE TO DEFEND ME.
WE'LL CER-TAINLY TRY.
EN GARDE, MORIARTY.
YOU DARE CHALLENGE ME??
NOW YOU'LL SEE!!!
IS THAT HOW THAT WRETCH STOLE THE EXCALIBUR? HMMM...
...LET ME THINK.
YOU'D BETTER DO IT QUICKLY BECAUSE ZACHARY COULD BE IN DANGER.
HMMM... I DON'T THINK SO. WE HAVE PLENTY OF TIME.
DIANA, MERLIN, IF YOU DON'T HURRY A BIT, THIS COULD FINISH BADLY.

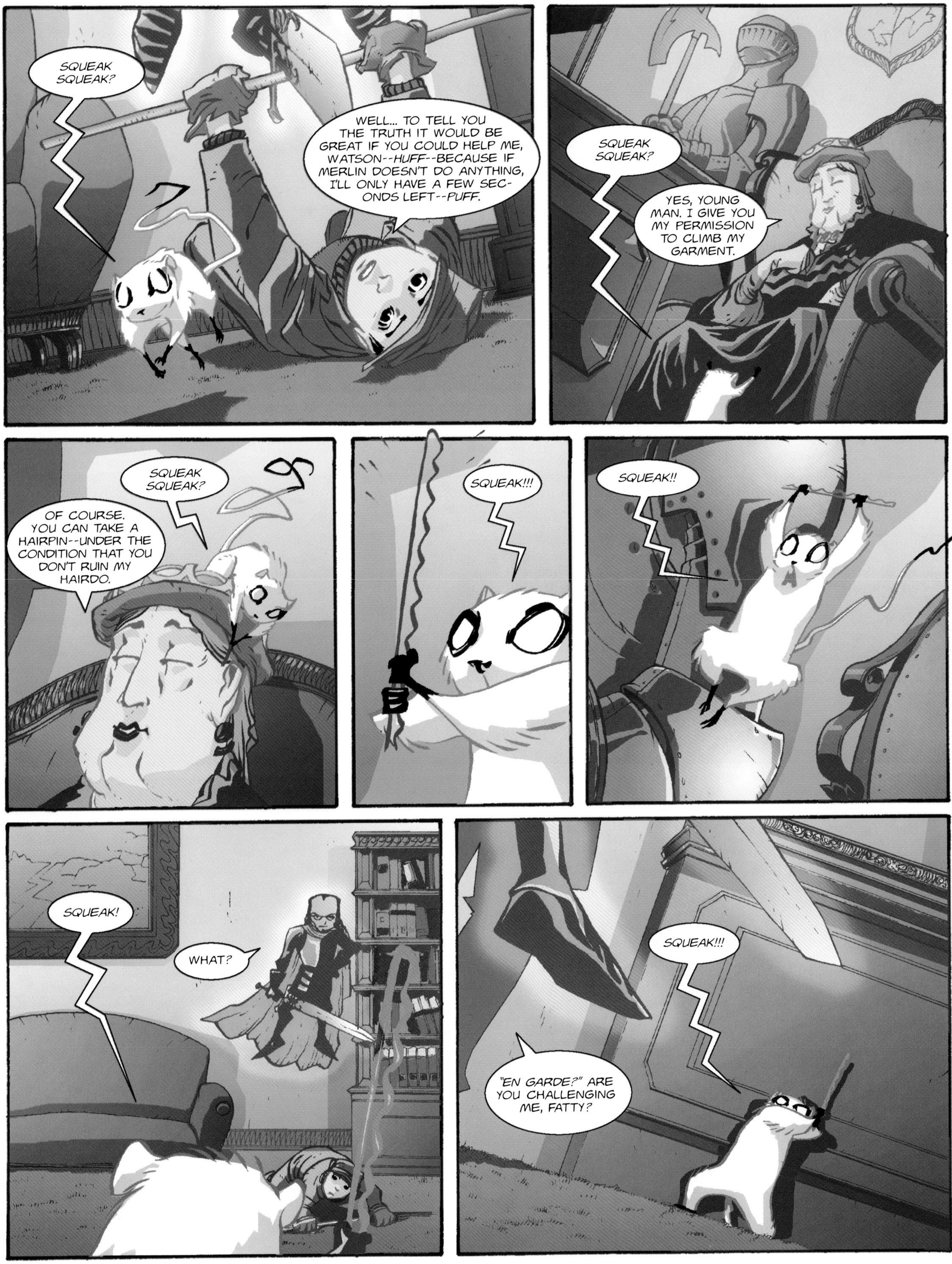
SQUEAK SQUEAK?
WELL... TO TELL YOU THE TRUTH IT WOULD BE GREAT IF YOU COULD HELP ME, WATSON--HUFF--BECAUSE IF MERLIN DOESN'T DO ANYTHING, I'LL ONLY HAVE A FEW SEC-ONDS LEFT--PUFF.
SQUEAK SQUEAK?
YES, YOUNG MAN. I GIVE YOU MY PERMISSION TO CLIMB MY GARMENT.
SQUEAK SQUEAK?
OF COURSE. YOU CAN TAKE A HAIRPIN--UNDER THE CONDITION THAT YOU DON'T RUIN MY HAIRDO.
SQUEAK!!!
SQUEAK!!
SQUEAK!
WHAT?
SQUEAK!!!
"EN GARDE?" ARE YOU CHALLENGING ME, FATTY?

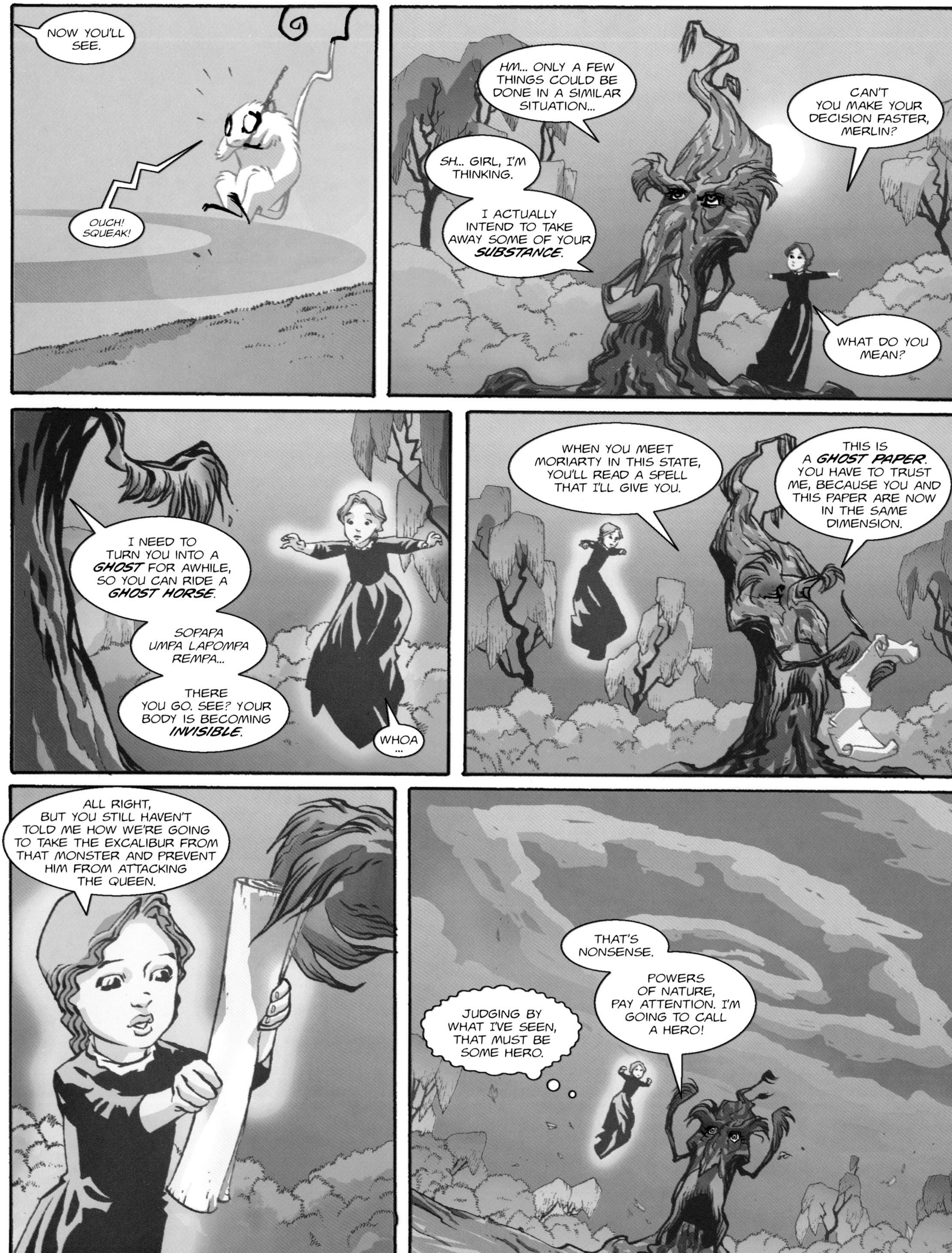
NOW YOU'LL SEE.
OUCH! SQUEAK!
HM... ONLY A FEW THINGS COULD BE DONE IN A SIMILAR SITUATION...
SH... GIRL, I'M THINKING.
I ACTUALLY INTEND TO TAKE AWAY SOME OF YOUR SUBSTANCE.
CAN'T YOU MAKE YOUR DECISION FASTER, MERLIN?
WHAT DO YOU MEAN?
I NEED TO TURN YOU INTO A GHOST FOR AWHILE, SO YOU CAN RIDE A GHOST HORSE.
SOPAPA UMPA LAPOMPA REMPA...
THERE YOU GO. SEE? YOUR BODY IS BECOMING INVISIBLE.
WHOA ...
WHEN YOU MEET MORIARTY IN THIS STATE, YOU'LL READ A SPELL THAT I'LL GIVE YOU.
THIS IS A GHOST PAPER. YOU HAVE TO TRUST ME, BECAUSE YOU AND THIS PAPER ARE NOW IN THE SAME DIMENSION.
ALL RIGHT, BUT YOU STILL HAVEN'T TOLD ME HOW WE'RE GOING TO TAKE THE EXCALIBUR FROM THAT MONSTER AND PREVENT HIM FROM ATTACKING THE QUEEN.
THAT'S NONSENSE.
POWERS OF NATURE, PAY ATTENTION. I'M GOING TO CALL A HERO!
JUDGING BY WHAT I'VE SEEN, THAT MUST BE SOME HERO.

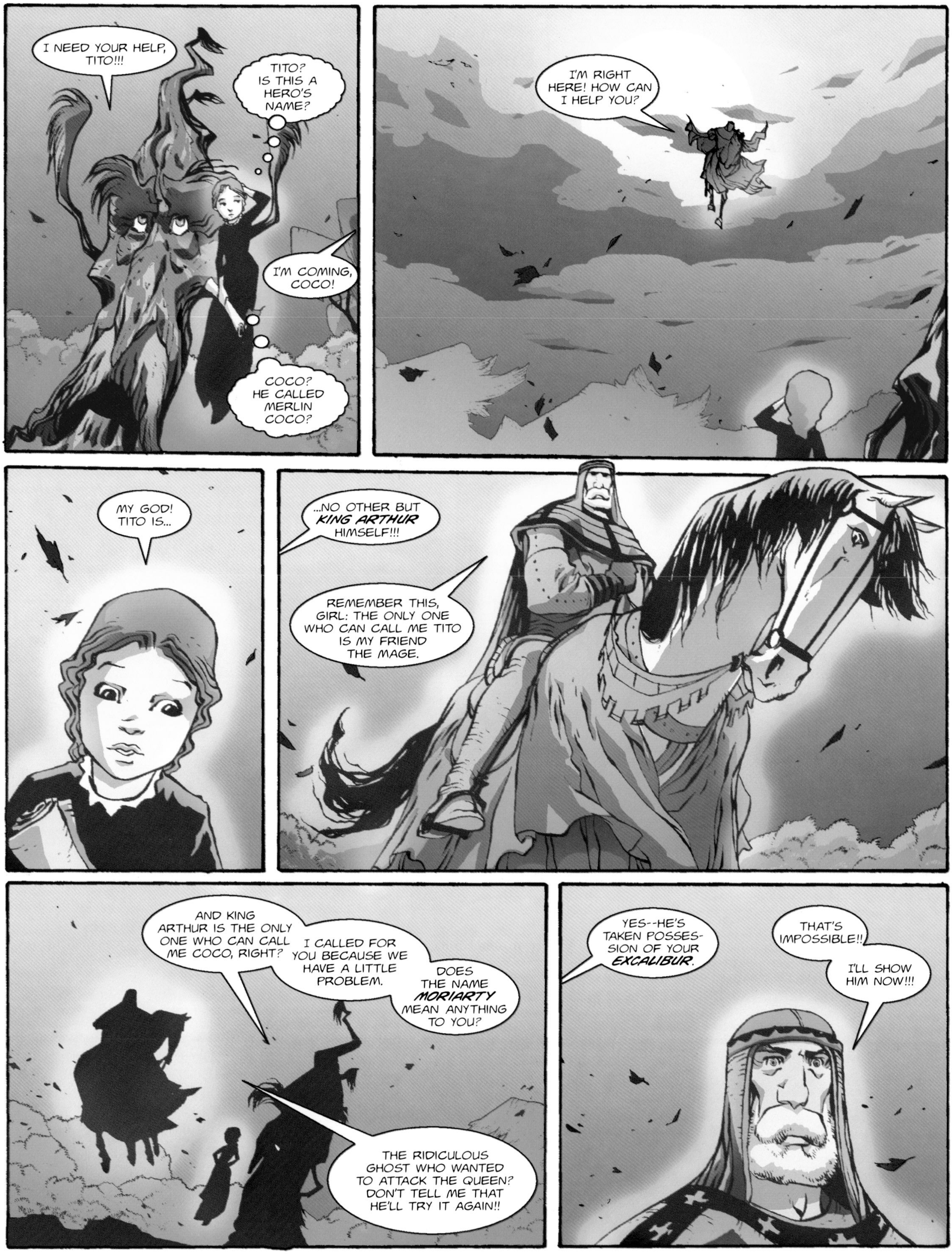
I NEED YOUR HELP, TITO!!!
TITO? IS THIS A HERO'S NAME?
I'M COMING, COCO!
COCO? HE CALLED MERLIN COCO?
I'M RIGHT HERE! HOW CAN I HELP YOU?
MY GOD! TITO IS...
...NO OTHER BUT ***KING ARTHUR*** HIMSELF!!!
REMEMBER THIS, GIRL: THE ONLY ONE WHO CAN CALL ME TITO IS MY FRIEND THE MAGE.
AND KING ARTHUR IS THE ONLY ONE WHO CAN CALL ME COCO, RIGHT?
I CALLED FOR YOU BECAUSE WE HAVE A LITTLE PROBLEM.
DOES THE NAME ***MORIARTY*** MEAN ANYTHING TO YOU?
THE RIDICULOUS GHOST WHO WANTED TO ATTACK THE QUEEN? DON'T TELL ME THAT HE'LL TRY IT AGAIN!!
YES--HE'S TAKEN POSSESSION OF YOUR ***EXCALIBUR***.
THAT'S IMPOSSIBLE!!
I'LL SHOW HIM NOW!!!

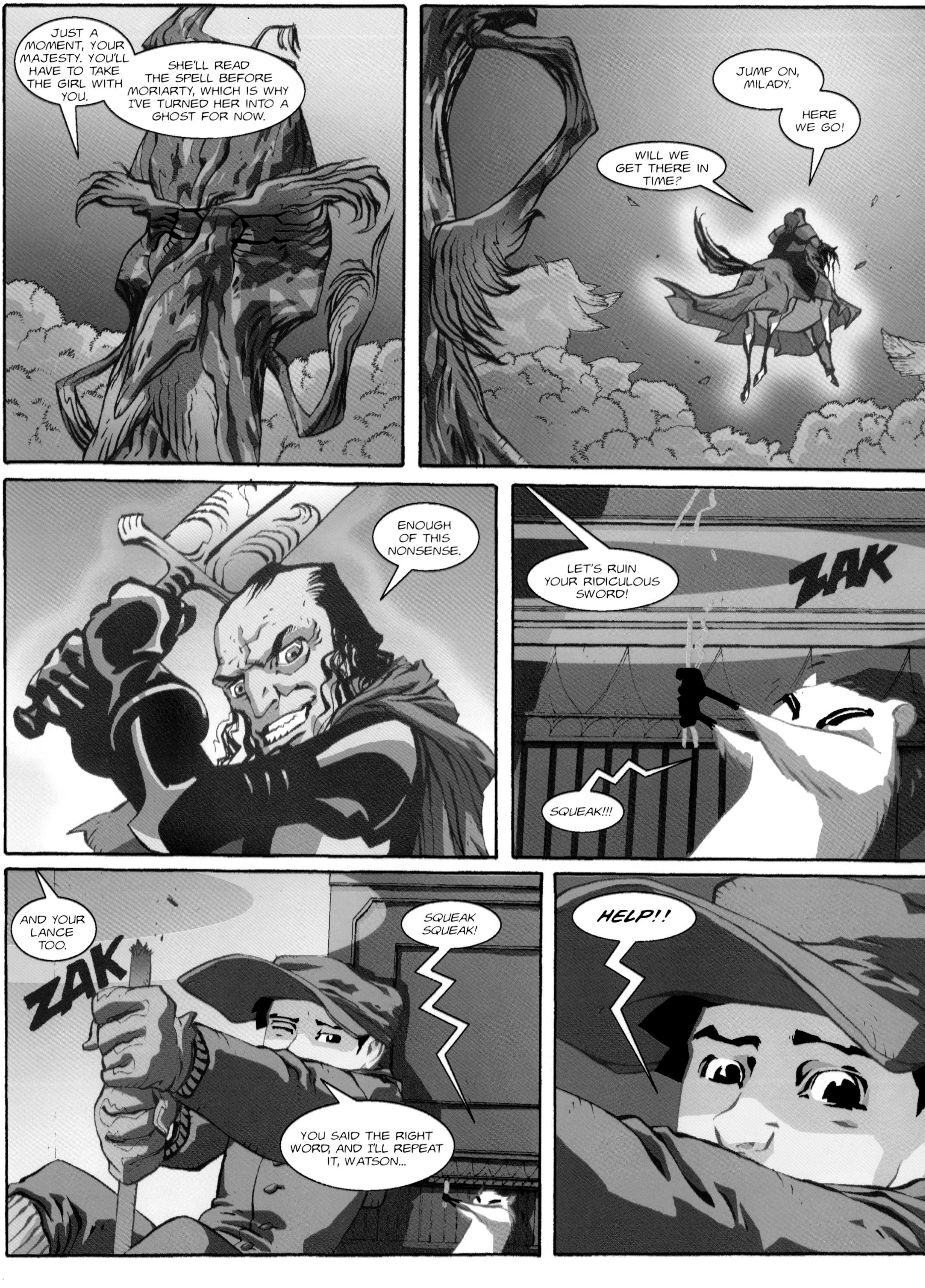
JUST A MOMENT, YOUR MAJESTY. YOU'LL HAVE TO TAKE THE GIRL WITH YOU.
SHE'LL READ THE SPELL BEFORE MORIARTY, WHICH IS WHY I'VE TURNED HER INTO A GHOST FOR NOW.
JUMP ON, MILADY.
HERE WE GO!
WILL WE GET THERE IN TIME?
ENOUGH OF THIS NONSENSE.
LET'S RUIN YOUR RIDICULOUS SWORD!
ZAK
SQUEAK!!!
AND YOUR LANCE TOO.
ZAK
SQUEAK SQUEAK!
YOU SAID THE RIGHT WORD, AND I'LL REPEAT IT, WATSON...
HELP!!

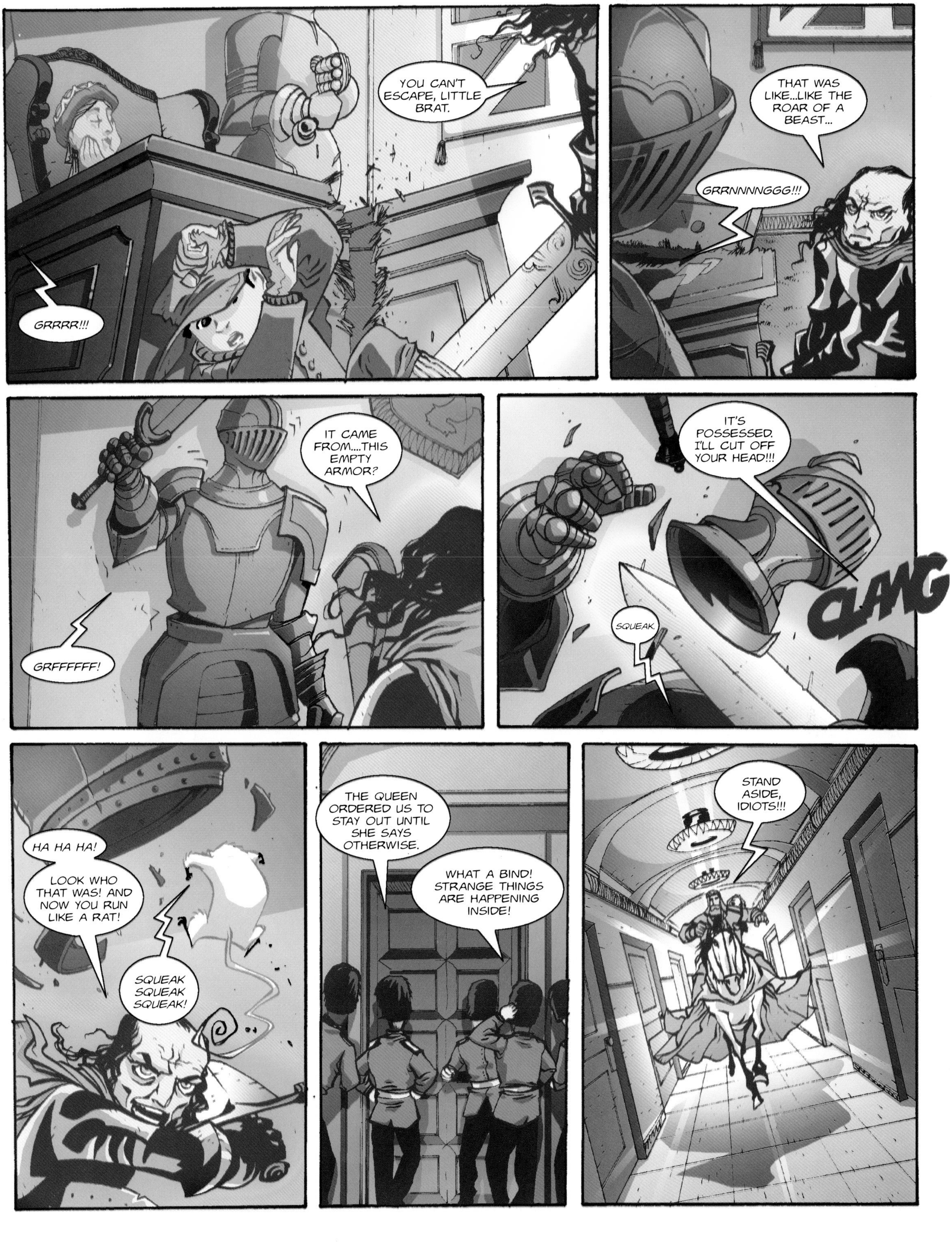
YOU CAN'T ESCAPE, LITTLE BRAT.
GRRRR!!!
THAT WAS LIKE...LIKE THE ROAR OF A BEAST...
GRRNNNNGGG!!!
IT CAME FROM....THIS EMPTY ARMOR?
GRFFFFFF!
IT'S POSSESSED. I'LL CUT OFF YOUR HEAD!!!
SQUEAK.
CLANG
HA HA HA!
LOOK WHO THAT WAS! AND NOW YOU RUN LIKE A RAT!
SQUEAK SQUEAK SQUEAK!
THE QUEEN ORDERED US TO STAY OUT UNTIL SHE SAYS OTHERWISE.
WHAT A BIND! STRANGE THINGS ARE HAPPENING INSIDE!
STAND ASIDE, IDIOTS!!!

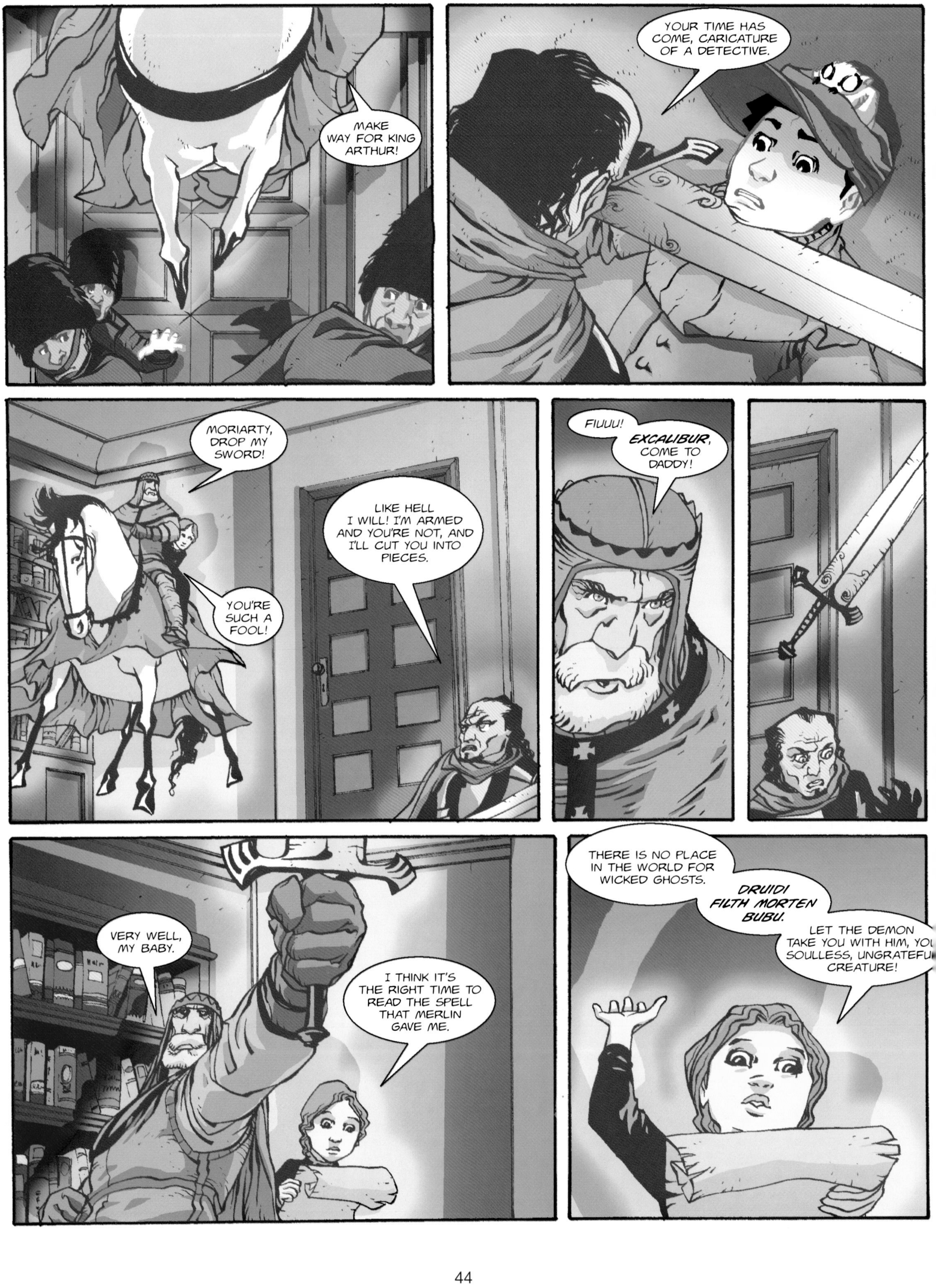
MAKE WAY FOR KING ARTHUR!
YOUR TIME HAS COME, CARICATURE OF A DETECTIVE.
MORIARTY, DROP MY SWORD!
LIKE HELL I WILL! I'M ARMED AND YOU'RE NOT, AND I'LL CUT YOU INTO PIECES.
YOU'RE SUCH A FOOL!
FIUUU! EXCALIBUR, COME TO DADDY!
VERY WELL, MY BABY.
I THINK IT'S THE RIGHT TIME TO READ THE SPELL THAT MERLIN GAVE ME.
THERE IS NO PLACE IN THE WORLD FOR WICKED GHOSTS.
DRUIDI FILTH MORTEN BUBU.
LET THE DEMON TAKE YOU WITH HIM, YOU SOULLESS, UNGRATEFUL CREATURE!

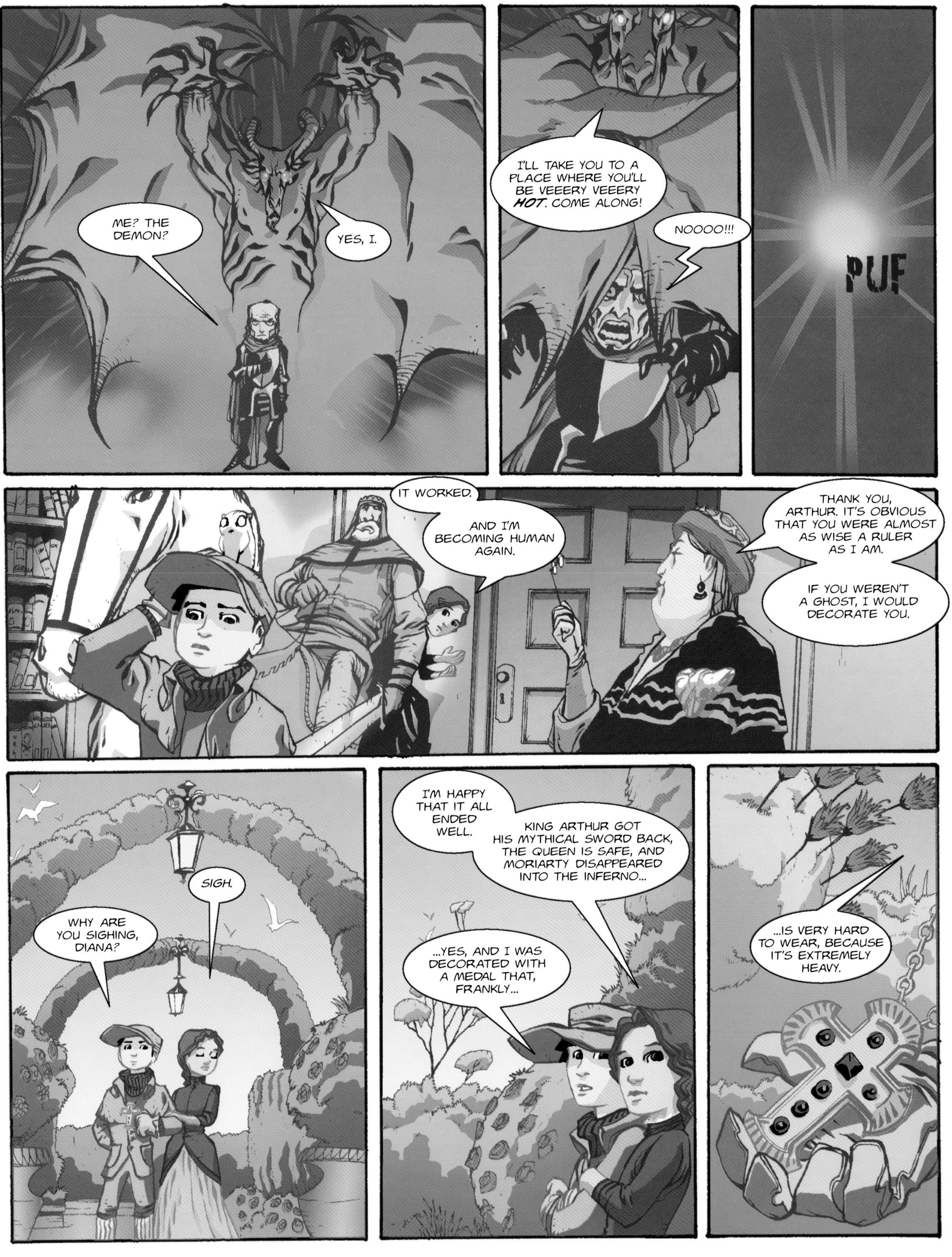
ME? THE DEMON?
YES, I.
I'LL TAKE YOU TO A PLACE WHERE YOU'LL BE VEEERY VEEERY *HOT*. COME ALONG!
NOOOO!!!
PUF
IT WORKED.
AND I'M BECOMING HUMAN AGAIN.
THANK YOU, ARTHUR. IT'S OBVIOUS THAT YOU WERE ALMOST AS WISE A RULER AS I AM.
IF YOU WEREN'T A GHOST, I WOULD DECORATE YOU.
SIGH.
WHY ARE YOU SIGHING, DIANA?
I'M HAPPY THAT IT ALL ENDED WELL.
KING ARTHUR GOT HIS MYTHICAL SWORD BACK, THE QUEEN IS SAFE, AND MORIARTY DISAPPEARED INTO THE INFERNO...
...YES, AND I WAS DECORATED WITH A MEDAL THAT, FRANKLY...
...IS VERY HARD TO WEAR, BECAUSE IT'S EXTREMELY HEAVY.

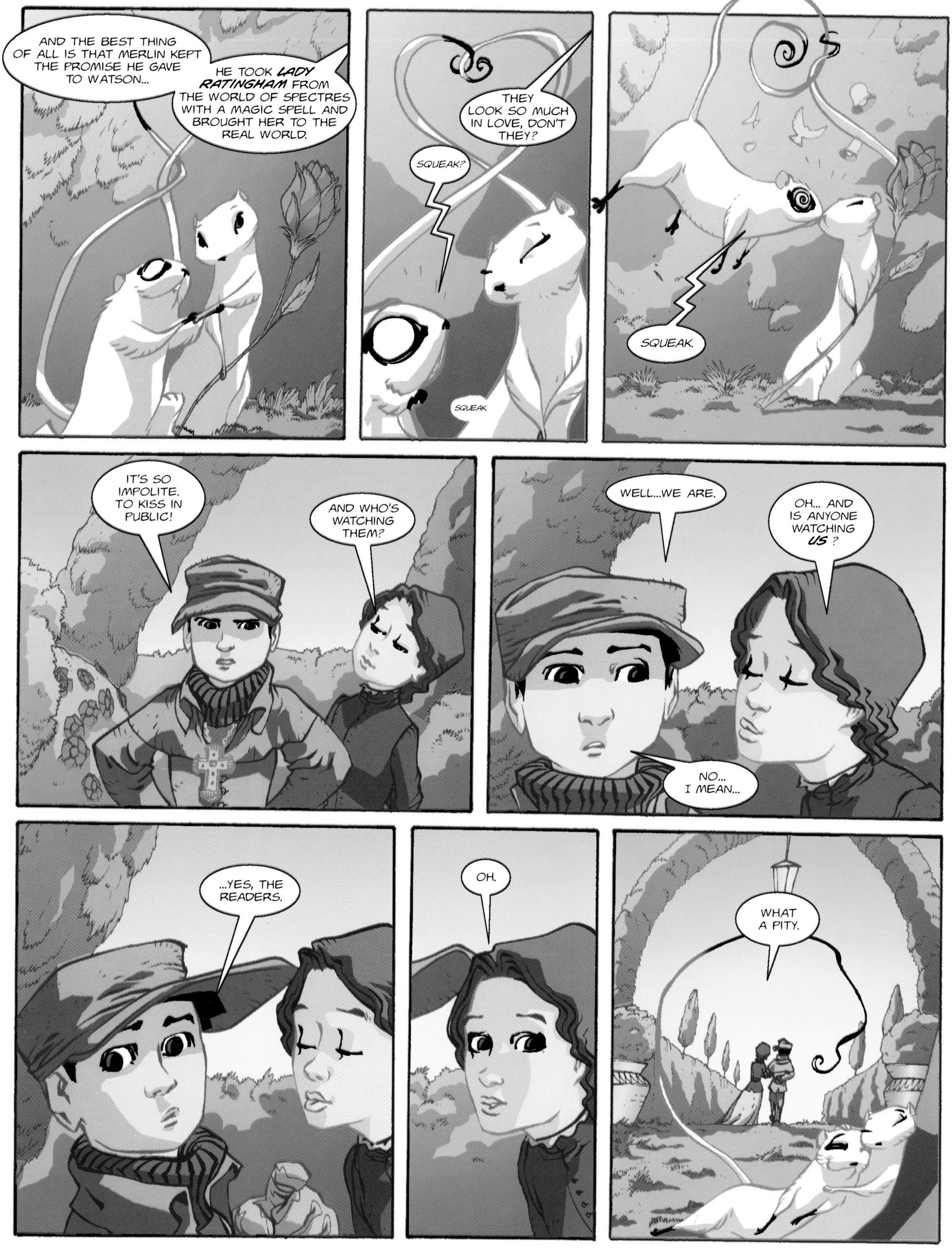
AND THE BEST THING OF ALL IS THAT MERLIN KEPT THE PROMISE HE GAVE TO WATSON...
HE TOOK LADY RATINGHAM FROM THE WORLD OF SPECTRES WITH A MAGIC SPELL AND BROUGHT HER TO THE REAL WORLD.
THEY LOOK SO MUCH IN LOVE, DON'T THEY?
SQUEAK?
SQUEAK
SQUEAK.
IT'S SO IMPOLITE. TO KISS IN PUBLIC!
AND WHO'S WATCHING THEM?
WELL...WE ARE.
OH... AND IS ANYONE WATCHING US ?
NO... I MEAN...
...YES, THE READERS.
OH.
WHAT A PITY.

THE END

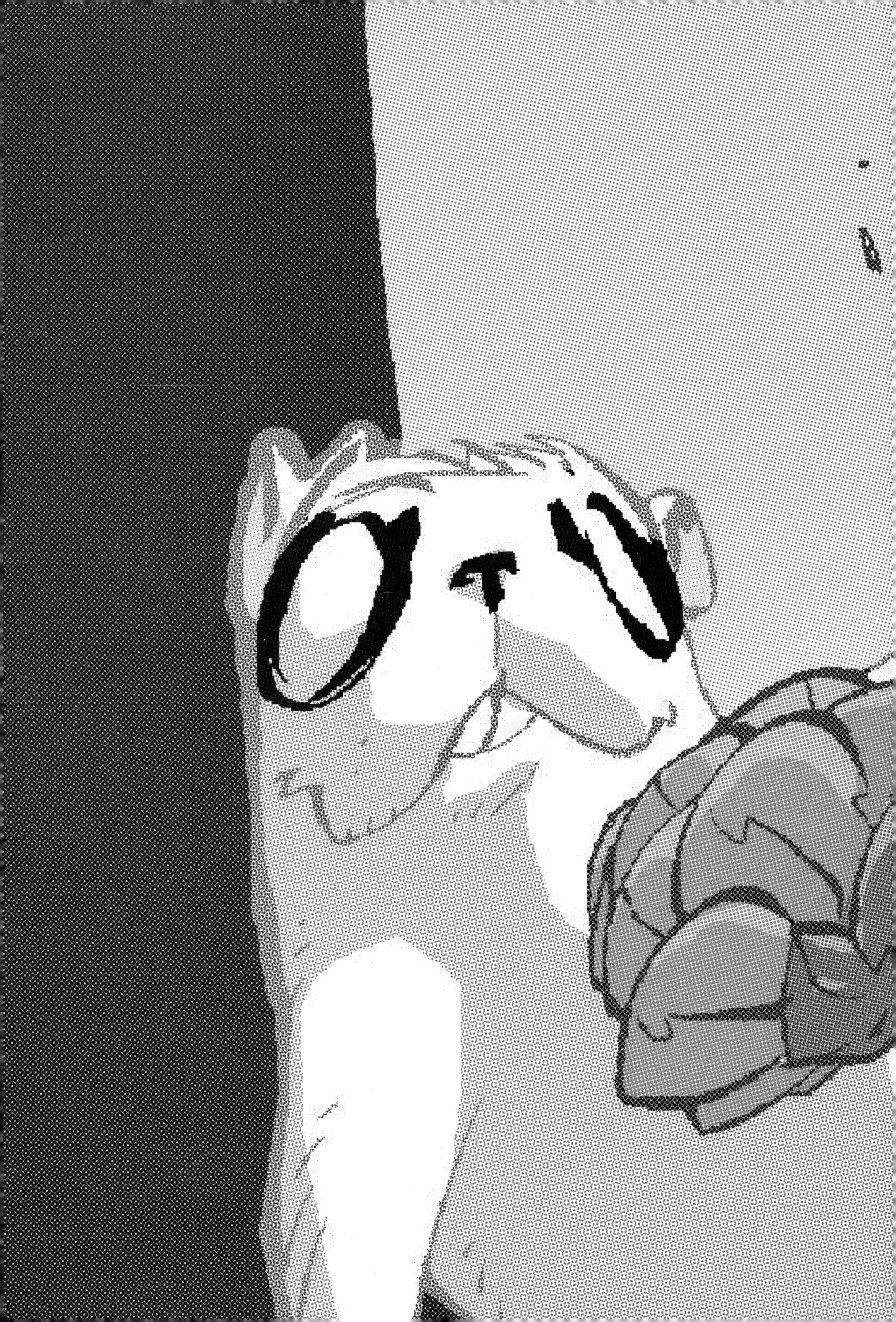